Take Them
by
the Hand

A Leadership Guide For Coaches

Jeffrey Usher

ISBN 978-0-9762014-3-7

Scripture quotations are taken from the Revised Standard Version (RSV) of the Bible, copyright 1952 [2nd edition, 1971] by the Division of Christian Education of the National Council of the Churches of Christ in the United States of America. Used by permission. All rights reserved.

Published by L'Edge Press
A division of Upside Down Ministries, Inc.
P.O. Box 2567
Boone, North Carolina
1.877.262.0036

Dedication

This book is dedicated to the three most important people in my life, my wife and two children.

My son, Zachary and my daughter, Emily gave me the opportunity and reason to be involved in coaching and ministry in the first place. Their patience, tolerance and willingness to let me be their coach, not only once, but over and over again have been blessings to me. Zach's compassion for others and his pursuit of justice continually renew my faith in the next generation. Emily's smile and sense of humor remind me that life is truly unfolding as it should.

Candice, my wife of more than twenty-five years has chosen to love me just the way I am. Not only has she allowed me to take the time to coach and play with the kids each week, but she has encouraged it. For my never ending stream of "ideas" about practice, games and devotionals, she has been a constant source of feedback and a beacon guiding me along my way. Her unconditional love gives me the courage to keep trying in my own unique way.

For me, to be a coach is a wonderful thing. But to be a husband to Candice and a dad to Zach and Emi has been my dream come true and the reason I live.

Table of Contents

Sharing My Gifts: A Call to Service

All know the way; few actually walk it
—Zen Saying

Of all the things we do in our lives, as adults and parents, the most important may be to teach and guide our children. Like our parents before us, we must show them how to be good people and become valuable members of society. It is our responsibility. It is our duty. It is the "way of the world"—to take what we have learned and pass it on to the next generation.

I believe we must teach our children about values, character and love. We must show them how to play by the rules. We must show them how to be competitive, yet compassionate. We must show them how to build relationships and love each other. In a larger sense, if we are to ever address issues like war and peace, hunger and disease, and religious differences, we must first do our part at home where we know we have a chance to make an impact.

There are many ways to pass it on, but they all include spending time with our children; listening to them; and showing them we care. There are many activities that can be used to nurture our children in many similar ways, but I believe adults are most effective when we try to lead them in our own ways, using our own unique gifts and talents. I think I have found my way using youth soccer. So, for many years I have gone to the soccer fields to "nurture others"—over and over again.

I have coached more than 40 soccer and basketball teams in a faith-based youth recreational league over the past 10 years. My dream has been to do my part by teaching the lessons of character and team work without taking away the fun or competition of these games.

We all know that a very small percentage of children who participate in sports will end up as professional athletes. Most will only use sports as recreation. A source of fun, a source of fellowship, a way to exercise their bodies. A way to blow off steam. But, I have discovered there are great opportunities within these play times to teach the lessons of life.

Leading young people is a huge responsibility. For three hours or so each week, parents entrust their children with me to give them direction, to build their bodies, to influence their minds and their spirits. I have learned that my opportunity to influence these children is tremendous. So, I no longer take my responsibility lightly.

From giving five-year-olds their first impression of what sports are all about, to helping thirteen-year-old girls compete with 15-year-old boys, to helping 18-year-old boys deal with being tough while still being good sports, the potential to guide them is huge. But, the ever present question is: "Will WE choose to lead them?" If we do not, WHO will? I believe those of us who know the way MUST accept our responsibility to lead those who will follow.

I have been told by players, parents and opposing coaches that my approach to coaching sports is a gift. I have been told that I build confidence in individual players, and that I build teams that care about each individual. I have been told that I help kids understand that the numbers on the scoreboard are not the only measures that count in their lives. I have been told that I emphasize values and character for those who play for me. I have been told that I show love for my players and in return they come to love me.

For years, I have shared my gift with players, coaches and parents one team at a time. Some of those who have gone with me before have urged me to share what I have experienced with others. So, this book is my attempt to share with those others who also desire to make a difference by leading young people.

I am not a trained pastor, youth minister or educator. What I share is based on my real life experiences—successes and failures. This book is not about coaching just to win (although there may be places for that). This book is about using sports to build relationships and to make better people. This book is a "call to service" to those who feel the need to "do their part" and pass on the lessons of life.

I have been lucky enough to discover some secrets that have helped me along the way. As you will see, I call them my "stepping stones." By sharing, I hope others may use some of what I have found, along with their own God-given talents, to touch the lives of the ones who are the hope for the future - our kids.

As I look back, I can see that there are ten steps I have taken season after season when trying to lead the children. My steps look like this:

MY STEPPING STONES
1. Making a Commitment
2. Having a Dream
3. Finding the Steps
4. Taking the Lead
5. Knowing Your Followers
6. Taking the Steps
7. Shining the Light
8. Encouraging Others
9. Keeping Your Balance
10. Showing Them the Way

I have learned my lessons from starts, restarts, mistakes, do overs, and gentle counseling from others. I know I am not smarter or more clever than others; but, I have had the opportunity to make my mistakes earlier (and perhaps more often) than those who may choose to follow after me. So, if I share, perhaps others will be able to move on faster than I did, get over some of the obstacles more easily and get onto leading the kids. So, I want to share the "stepping stones" that allowed me to find my way.

This book is a collection of my experiences. There are stories, devotionals, poems, some perspective and some philosophy. In many places I have revealed myself and shown what is in my heart. In the final analysis, it seems all I really have to give is what has been put in my heart. After all, isn't that the greatest gift we have to pass on?

By the end, I hope this collection of experiences all comes together for you as it has for me—as a "series of steps" you can follow when you decide to take others by the hand and lead them.

Author's Note: This book is truly a collection of my experience. Please bear with me when I tell you that at times, I have combined more than one story. As I have reflected upon years gone by, some of the details may have faded in my memory a bit. At other times I have changed names and circumstances to help me explain the lessons I have learned. While I have taken the liberty to protect the identity of some persons, to embellish in some places and exaggerate in others, I have sought to keep the spirit of the experiences the same.

Is There A Prize Inside?

"Why have you come to draw up for battle?"
—1 Samuel 17[1]

Do you want to coach sports as the way you do your part in "passing it on" to our children? Why?

Along my journey, I have often asked that question of myself. "Why am I doing this?" Why am I coaching kids' soccer? Why am I here very week? As a grown man, why do I run around in short pants and soccer cleats? Why do I get so excited about a great pass, or jump up and down when a 5-year-old finally kicks the ball out of the proverbial "cluster" and puts it in the goal? There is no money in it. There is little public recognition. As a father and husband with children and a career and a home to take care of, certainly I do not do this to fill in my spare time.

So why? Part of the reason I wrote this book was to answer that question for myself. As I told my stories, I looked for the reasons. By writing, I found my answers. As I found my answers, I discovered more about myself. I could see who I am and what gifts I have to give. Understanding that has made a difference for me as well as the others in my life. Knowing that I can make a difference (no matter how small) has allowed to me go forward boldly. Perhaps you can use this book to help you answer your questions and find yourself.

During recent years, I coached two soccer teams each fall. One for my daughter who is twelve as I write this and one team for my son who is now nineteen. I coach the same combination in the spring. In between, in the winter, they both play basketball; so our routine is the same. I coach six teams a year. Fall, winter and spring, with practice, games, volunteer refereeing, and preparation time, I spend about ten hours each week on soccer or basketball.

All that time, all that energy. Why do I do it? Like a box of Cracker Jack, is there a prize inside? I think there is, so I have kept looking. Each season I open another box and sort through the peanuts and popcorn until I find the prize. Each season, I have found at least one surprise—and each of them has been worth looking for.

If you decide to go forward and look for the prize, here are the questions I would ask you to consider. Are you here just to coach a sport? To win or lose? Or, is there something else that motivates you? What is your real purpose for being here? What results do you want from your efforts?

I can not tell you what your answers should be, anymore than you can tell me why I should go on coaching. We each have to answer those questions for ourselves.

I use the story of David and Goliath often and for a number of purposes. It is a story that everyone knows, that teaches many lessons and never seems to get old. In this context, I point to the time when Goliath first comes onto the battlefield. In so many words, he yells across the field to the Israelites, "Why have you come to do battle today?" There is silence until David finally approaches and states his purpose. He boldly replies, "Because of what I do here today, all the world will know there is a God in Israel!"

David knew his purpose.

Why have you come to do battle? When your battle is finished, what will others know? As coaches, we can and should use sports for a larger and more meaningful purpose.

If we have courage like David, there is so much we can do.

STEPPING STONES

Why have you come to do battle?

Have you heard a "call to service?"

Who is on the team that you want to lead?

Where do you want to lead your team?

How will you know when you get there?

Making

a

Commitment

The difference is made
by the people who show up

The first step in the journey is to make a commitment. I made a decision to work with kids years ago. I made a commitment to help them become better people while having fun. I knew I had the gifts to help them; I just needed to make up my mind to do it.

But, I also knew I would need help. I have been lucky that others have helped me while I tried to lead the kids along the way. I have been thankful for the support of others as I have sometimes struggled to keep my commitment.

Through it all, my steadfast commitment has made my journey possible. You must decide whether you can make the commitment that is necessary to complete your own journey.

"Here I am Lord,
Is it I, Lord?
I have heard you calling in the night.
I will go, Lord, if you lead me.
I will hold your people in my heart."

—The United Methodist Hymnal[2]

Get Down Off Your Horse

"For I the Lord your God, hold your right hand;
it is I who say to you, fear not, I will help you."

—Isaiah 41[3]

I start with a story that has helped put it all in perspective for me. It tells about beginning the journey and making the commitment to lead others. The story envisions a league like ours where encouragement, sportsmanship and caring about other players are principles we live by. The story is a fairy tale—with a knight and a castle—and, the league is called the Kingdom. It goes like this:

Long ago there was a man named Coach Jeff who longed to be a soccer coach in the place known as the Kingdom. You see, Coach Jeff had heard of this kingdom where coaches and players encouraged each other, played with good sportsmanship and, above all, loved each other as children of God. So, one day, Coach Jeff set out in search of this wonderful place. He traveled near and far looking for the kingdom.

As he traveled, he asked the people he would meet in every village if they knew of the kingdom. As he questioned people along his way, he found that many had heard of the kingdom. Some thought they knew where it was and some even offered descriptions of this mystical place. But for days and days, Coach Jeff could not find the kingdom.

Finally one day, he came upon a village where the townspeople seemed certain the kingdom was somewhere nearby. Many townspeople offered him encouragement in his quest. Finally, one old gentleman offered Coach Jeff specific directions about how to get to there.

His directions went like this:"At the edge of the village, you will find a trail. Follow the trail into the woods until it splits. At the fork, go to the right until you come to the end. There at the trail's end, you will find the kingdom you seek."

More excited than ever, Coach Jeff set out on what he thought was the final leg of his journey. As he left the village, he found the path and followed it into the woods. Soon he came upon the fork, just as the old gentleman had said. Following his instructions, he took the path to the right and followed it to the end. However, much to his dismay, the path ended abruptly at the bank of a river. This river looked wide and Coach Jeff was certain that he could not cross it. Worse than that, the kingdom was nowhere in sight.

Looking across the wide river, Coach Jeff gathered his emotions. He thought he had come the right way, but perhaps he had made a mistake. His head hanging in disappointment, he wondered what to do next.

He stood there thinking, "all I want is to find this place where people encourage each other, where everyone plays by the rules and each one loves the other." He thought to himself. "I have tried so hard. I have traveled so far. I have asked for help. I have followed the directions that others have given to me. What else am I to do?"

Dejected, Coach Jeff turned away from the river and started back down the path. Just as he did, he heard a noise behind him. When he turned, he saw a knight on a great white horse coming from the woods. As he approached, the knight looked down and said, "Can I be of service to you?" Looking up, Coach Jeff replied, "I have come in search of a kingdom full of encouragement, fair play and love. Although I have followed the directions given to me, I can not seem to find the wonderful place."

As a smile came across his face, the knight jumped down from his horse and stood before Coach Jeff. The knight reached out and took Coach Jeff by his hand. He then turned and led him a short distance to a spot along the bank of the river. There, still holding Coach Jeff's hand, he stepped into the river.

Unsure about what was happening at first, Coach Jeff looked down at where the knight had stepped into the water. As he took his first steps, Coach Jeff could see that at that point in the river, there were stepping stones just beneath the surface. For someone who knew the way, there was a line of stones leading to the other side. So, holding the knight's hand firmly, Coach Jeff walked confidently and safely across the water to the far side.

As Coach Jeff stepped on the opposite bank, he could see for the first time a castle in the valley below. "That", said the knight, "is the kingdom you seek."

The knight and Coach Jeff walked into the valley and entered the castle where they found a wonderful feast going on. Many people were eating, drinking, and enjoying good fellowship. The others asked Coach Jeff to join them. And so he did.

At the head of the table sat a great Wizard - a large man with a beard. After the meal was finished, the great Wizard said to Coach Jeff, "Now that you have come so far and found our kingdom, tell us what you have learned."

After gathering his thoughts, Coach Jeff responded that in his quest to find this place where he could be part of the encouragement, caring and love he desired, he found that many people had heard of this kingdom. He found that many people knew this place was good. Many thought they knew where it was and some even offered directions on how to get here. But try as he might, in the end, he could not find his way until someone got down off his horse, took him by the hand and showed him the way.

To that, the great Wizard replied, "Well done, Coach Jeff. You have learned your lesson well. Now, you, too know the secret of this place. So from this day forward, wherever you go or whatever you do; when you come upon someone who needs encouragement or who needs caring or love; you may no longer simply tell them what to do, or give them directions; but now, you, too must get down off your horse, take them by the hand and show them the way."

In this world, there are many people who know what needs to be done. Among them are those who can give direction. But it seems to me the people who are really making a difference are the ones who make the commitment to "get off their horses", take others by the hand and show them the way.

Like many, when I began coaching, I was fortunate enough to have a few knights take me by the hand and show me the way. Once it was a head coach allowing me to help in his practices. Once it was an assistant coach putting his hand on my shoulder and showing me what to say in my devotionals. Once it was the league director leading me through a disciplinary situation with a player. It has always been my wife showing me a better way.

Now, it is me gently showing a player to his position on the field. Now, it is me in practice trying my best to show them how to make a corner kick. Now, it is me standing in the pouring rain while my high school team finishes a game and showing that I care.

I have learned that if we are committed to our journeys, sooner or later, someone will come along take us by the hand, and show us what we can not do ourselves. We must be thankful when they do. We must watch, listen and learn everything we can from them. You see, they have walked down the path before. They have found the stepping stones. They know the way across the water and they have been sent to show us.

Once we have found our way, we must be willingly to go back and show the others. They are waiting for us!

STEPPING STONES

Before you take the first step, you must make a commitment to the journey.

Are you willing to make the commitment of "getting down off your horse and taking others by the hand?"

As Much as I Ever Will

"...but the greatest of these is LOVE."
—1 Corinthians 13[4]

God loves us unconditionally and expects us to do the same to others. As coaches, when we make a commitment to lead the children, we must act as His disciples and make the commitment to love our players as God loves us. The scripture says that love endures all things and that love never ends. If we are to be role models and lead our children, this is one of the lessons we must pass on to them. We must show our unconditional commitment to them. How do we do that? Here's an example I used to help my players understand one season.

Years ago, when we first got married, my wife and I attended a large church in Oklahoma City. The pastor was a wonderful man and one of the most eloquent preachers I have ever experienced. I remember being especially taken by the way he performed the baptism of babies. As he held a young child in his arms, he would say, "Today God loves you. Today, He loves you as much as He ever will; and, nothing you can do will ever make Him love you any more or any less than He does at this moment!" With these few words, the pastor summed up the spirit of God's unconditional love for each of His children!

I was able to extend that story and show my own commitment to my own players. At the beginning of the season, I purchased a package of note cards. I wrote a short note to each player on my team. Each read like this:

Dear Emily;
You are a special player.
Thank you for being on our team this season.
Love, Coach Jeff
After writing the same short note for each one, I addressed the

envelopes, sealed them and put them in my desk drawer for the rest of the season.

At our end-of-the-season gathering, I told the players the story about my pastor in Oklahoma. I told them that as their coach, I had tried to act as a disciple and to love them without question. I then gave them each the sealed envelope with their name on it.

I told them, that before the first game...before I knew how many games we would win or lose, before I knew how many goals any of them would score, before I knew how many other good plays each of them would make; OR before I knew how many mistakes any of us would make, I wrote them each one of these notes.

I told them the note says that you are special. It says that I love you. Just like my pastor in Oklahoma, this note says that no matter what you did this season, my love for you did not change. I loved you for who you are....and, nothing that you did this season made me love you any more or any less than I did when I wrote you this note. As you leave this season, I will continue to love you and nothing you do will make me love you anymore or any less than I do today.

Then, I asked my players to do the same as me. I asked them to love others without regard to whether they are good soccer players or whether they are popular in school or what type clothes they wear. I asked the players to love each other as God has loved them, unconditionally.

We receive unconditional love from our God. He asks simply that we do the same for others. Find a way to "walk the talk"...a tangible way to show your love and commitment.

STEPPING STONES

Commitment to others means being LOYAL to them.

Name one person to whom you are LOYAL.

WHY are you loyal to that person?

Others will be loyal to you for the same reasons.

How can you start demonstrating the same kind of LOYALTY to your players?

Having

a

Dream

"...seek, and you will find..."
—Matthew 7[5]

If you are going to make a commitment, you need to know where your journey will lead. You need to have a vision of where you want to go. Are you going to chase a dream? Do you want to make the world a better place? Even if you can only change a small corner of it? Do you want to change lives? Even if you can only change a few?

Over time, I have developed a vision of my destination. It's simply the place I hope to find at the other end of the stepping stones! It's the place where I want to lead others. I have taken many steps in pursuit of my dream. I am not there, yet, but I know what my dream looks like, so I keep pursuing it.

Living My Dream

*"Every valley shall be filled, and every mountain and hill shall be
brought low; and the crooked shall be made straight and the rough
ways shall be made smooth."*

—Luke 3[6]

I have been blessed to be part of a wonderful sports league for all
the years that I have coached. It is a faith based league of
encouragement sponsored by the outreach ministry of a local church.
It is a league that is based on the principles of encouragement,
sportsmanship and fair play. We welcome all to play, even though we
share Christian principles and pray together often.

The league is as well run as any of the recreational leagues in our
large city, with beautiful playing fields, equipment and uniforms
second to none, and a quality of play that continually improves. I am
proud to be a part of this league.

Although it looks like many other leagues, there is something
more to it. It is a special place where I have learned as many lessons
as the players. On many occasions, I have tried to explain what makes
this league so special. Last year I was able to put the description in the
form of a poem. I think the poem captures the spirit of the league and
what it means to me.

Martin Luther King, Jr. encouraged us to have a dream. He
encouraged us to dream of a time and place where we all would join
together as brothers and sisters. He encouraged us to work to follow
his dream of how the world might be. Perhaps this is my dream about
how I wish the world could be—using our soccer fields as our starting
point. It is the vision that I keep pursuing.

Maybe what follows is not so much a poem ABOUT something as
much as it is my PRAYER FOR something. It describes the destination
where I hope my journey will end.

Living My Dream

In the town where we live is a place I adore
It looks like some others, but it is so much more

Soccer is one of the games that we play
The difference is not in the rules—but the way

When you enter in front, the gate it is narrow
A symbol of one of the lessons we borrow

The fields are all green and beautifully mowed
The results of the seeds we have carefully sowed

Balls are collected in bags on the ground
Anxiously waiting to be kicked up and down

Game time draws near, cars fill the lot
On this September Saturday, it's gonna be hot

The crowd—an assembly of family and friends
Who come with the spirit to cheer without end

And then comes the difference, the players, the kids
We call them God's children—our future, it's said

They run on the field full of laughter and fun
We hope they'll be happy, when this day is done

Their shirts full of color, their shoes sometimes muddy
Today some will likely oppose their best buddy

All meet in the center, the circle is grand
Two teams joined together, each one hand in hand

Thanks for the day and the chance to be there
Safety and fair play are all in their prayer

They have gifts and talents they all want to use
But no hitting or shoving or words of abuse

Like young David when facing Goliath, no less
In God's name they battle in their weekly test

They play with the spirit that God put inside
But their love for each other, they never do hide

They kick and they block and they pass and they score
But, the numbers don't matter, as we've seen before

The winning and losing are different, you see
They look a bit different upon victory

The ones who have won are the ones who have played
The victors are those whose best efforts were made

Those who play hard and remember the team
Are the ones who learned most of the lesson, it seems

From the fans, there's a word that they all like to hear
They encourage the players that they love so dear

Effort, and courage, and doing their best
Are the things that bring the most cheers from the rest

When the clock has run out and there's no time left
And the warm autumn sun slowly sets in the west

The two teams line up—tired, sweaty and muddy
And shake each other's hands—especially that buddy

They say"way to go","atta boy"and"nice game"

Pats on the back, as they call each by name

Then players, they circle around their own coach
As the daddies and grandmas and siblings approach

One of the moms brought a snack they can eat
A juice or a soda and a rice krispies treat

They laugh and they giggle and talk of the play
And fun that they've had on this bright sunny day

Coach David made note of good plays for the day
As he reads them, Coach Jeff sends some candy their way

Before it all ends, they join hands and bow heads
And give thanks to the one who has made them all friends

Go home quickly and safely, they say, and then
Bring them together next practice, again

As they each start to leave, as the sun warms each face
A spirit of peace seems to be in this place

A good day for all—the fans that you see
For players, for coaches and the game referee

The good Lord was with us, I have no doubt
The signs of His presence are all about

All sense the power that comes from above
Each one knows the feeling—it must be God's love

For, that one short hour is the time that we spend
When nothing else matters but family and friends

For a brief time on weekends in this crazy land
The Lord gives us comfort by the touch of His hand

These are the reasons I cherish this place
As I look at the smiles, I envision God's face

After so many seasons, I finally can see,
This is where God sends His blessings to me.

So I'll keep on coaching team after team
At this place full of hope, where I'm living my dream.

STEPPING STONES

Do you have a dream? What is it?

Do you know where you want to be at the end of your journey?

At the beginning of each season I make two lists that look like this:

My Goals for the Season	My Players' Goals for the Season
1. Have FUN	1. Have FUN
2. Make friends	2. Make a friend
3. Teach soccer	3. Learn about soccer
4. Share my faith	4. Be a good sport

Can you make a list that describes your goals?

Do you have the same goals as your players? Do your goals need to change?

The Starfish
and Losing in Overtime

"Never, never, never give up."
—Winston Churchill

There is a well known story about an old man walking on a beach. It was low tide and the exposed sand was covered with starfish for as far as the eye could see. As he walked along the beach, the man repeatedly bent over, picked up one of the starfish and threw it as far as he could back into the ocean water.

A younger man approached the old man as he took his morning walk from the opposite direction. As he came close to the old man, he asked, "Sir, I have been watching you toss starfish back into the ocean for quite some time as I walked. Why are you doing that?" The old man replied, "If the starfish lie on the sand until the next high tide, they will certainly die under the heat of the bright sun. If they are thrown back into the ocean water, they have a chance to survive." In a doubting tone, the young man asserted, "Look at all the hundreds of starfish that lay on this beach. Surely, you do not think one man can make such a difference."

Silently, the old man bent over once more, grabbed yet another starfish and hurled it far into the ocean. As he stood upright, he looked at the young man and confidently responded, "I made a difference for that one!"

A few years ago I was coaching a basketball game of third and fourth grade boys. It was a closely contested game. The tip off to start the second half went to one of the opposing players, who quickly dribbled to the foul line and put a beautiful jump shot in the bottom of the net! Unfortunately, it was the wrong basket. In the confusion that often comes when young teams switch ends of the court at halftime, the young boy had reacted as he had in the first half and shot at the same basket. The referee signaled for the basket to count and the points to be put on our side of the scoreboard.

Instinctively, I motioned to the ref to halt the action and I called him and the opposing coach to the side line. I explained that I understood what had happened. To avoid further embarrassment for the player, I suggested the points not be counted and that my team simply be awarded possession of the ball. We all agreed, the play resumed, and the miscue was soon forgotten.

As I sat back down, I wondered if I had done the right thing. I wondered to myself if I had just saved that player further embarrassment. Had the points counted, would he have been ridiculed by others including his own teammates? I wondered what if those points affect the outcome of the game. Would my players be disappointed? Did I do the right thing? Like the old man on the beach, was it worth it to make a difference for just one?

Often the impact of such decisions is not revealed for some time. But in this case the results came sooner than I expected. The game stayed close, so after regulation time ended in a tie, we played into overtime. At the end, our team lost by... you guessed it....two points. Those were the same two points I gave away to start the second half! That day, my act as a coach directly affected the outcome of the game. So, again, I asked myself, "Did I do the right thing?"

I believe when God closes a door, somewhere he opens a window. So, I took advantage of the situation at practice that week. We shared the story of the old man and the starfish. We talked about how my act of compassion had made a difference to the one player, even though it had a negative impact on our team. I asked the players to put themselves in the "shoes" of that player. I asked if they all hadn't made similar mistakes. I asked whether they would have welcomed a similar act of understanding and compassion. We asked ourselves which was more important, the feelings of the player or winning the game. We agreed that in this case making a difference for one was the right choice!

Do you see starfish who need a little "toss" to get back in the water? Is making a difference for one better than making no difference at all?

STEPPING STONES

Are you making a difference for just one player?

There are many "starfish" on the beach. We have to start somewhere. Perhaps others will see us and join in!

Run the Race Well

...“If you can meet with Triumph and Disaster
and treat those two Imposters just the same...”
—Rudyard Kipling[7]

What about winning and losing? Didn't Vince Lombardi tell us that "Winning isn't everything, it's the only thing"? Isn't that what sports are all about? Winning and losing? If it is not just a game, aren't the lessons about success and failure? Aren't the fields of competition where boys grow to be men and, nowadays where girls grow to be women? How can we not put winning first? How could we possibly play games and not keep score?

When I was growing up, we took Lombardi's words as gospel. As a teenage football player, that pretty much summed it up for me. Our coaches taught us to win. That's what they were supposed to do. Although we didn't realize it, the good coaches were also teaching us about character and values. But winning was always first.

Maybe Vince was right. We need to teach about winning and losing. But, we need to teach about character and values, too. One of my favorite quotes goes like this:

"Our job is to run the race well, God chooses who the winners are."

Take care of yourself. Run hard. Do your job well. Do your best. Won't the winning take care of itself?

There have been many great coaches in college and professional sports. Many have focused on winning and been successful. But it seems to me the ones who we admire the most, and the ones who have endured the longest are the ones who emphasized character, values and team along with winning. They are the ones who played by the rules. They are the ones who helped young people grow and mature in other ways.

In our state, Dean Smith is a living example of this philosophy. A man of impeccable character, values and integrity, he demanded the same of all his players. He taught them the values of life before he taught them the game of basketball. Yet, he coached at the University of North Carolina for 36 years and still holds the record for the most wins of any college basketball coach. His philosophy? Demand character, values, teamwork and the wins will take care of themselves. In his case, they did—his teams won 879 times!

As I look around our business world today, I see and read about many leaders who have made themselves and their companies into so-called winners. Large sales, huge profits. But, recently we have seen far too many of those same leaders involved in scandals and other inappropriate behavior. They have forgotten about integrity, values and character. They let winning be their only objective.

I see other leaders reading the headlines, then, scrambling for ways to put values back into their own organizations. Apparently, they too have figured out how to win, but, now, they are seeing the light. They have realized that for the long run, if their organizations are to prosper, they must be grounded on honesty, integrity and character.

So I ask this question, "Does it make more sense to teach character and values first and let the winning take care of itself?" In our fast paced, competitive, win-at-all-costs world, there are many places where our children are challenged with winning and losing. In the class room they receive grades for their efforts and are compared to others. They compete for selection into classes labeled "gifted", "talented" and "honors". In school plays, students try out for parts. Some win. Some lose. Parents begin the process early for their children when they compete for admission to the right preschool! The list of television shows where contestants compete for prizes ranging from money to husbands is long and growing. Videos games are just another example.

When parents tell me that their children need sports to teach them about winning and losing, I tell them, there are plenty of places their children already learn about those concepts. Our children are dealing with winning and losing everyday.

But, who is teaching them about values? What about character? And caring about others? If we agree that sports are such a great vehicle for learning, why don't we use them for teaching the most important lessons? I wonder, these days how many CEOs would welcome new employees who have already learned the lessons of character and teamwork. If new employees bring those values with them, surely the company can teach them how to 'score'.

In *Jesus, CEO*[8], Laurie Beth Jones tells the story of an athlete about to compete in a 100 yard dash at the Special Olympics. The young athlete had trained hard for many months and was excited about the race. When the gun sounded to start the race, the excitement of the moment overcame the young man. His arms flailed, his legs tangled and he fell to the ground just in front of the starting blocks.

All the other competitors were as eager as he to win the race. But, when they realized what had happened, one by one they stopped and returned to aid their fallen brother. After helping him to his feet, they all joined arms and walked the 100 yard distance together, crossing the finish line at the same time. The crowd cheered.

Ms. Jones says that Jesus had a rule for this situation. Nobody wins until we all do. She wonders what this world might be like if we all played by that one simple rule.

Nobody wins until we all do. I like that rule. Don't get me wrong, I love the competition as much as the next guy. I am proud when the scoreboard reads more on our side than the other. But, whose definition of winning are we using? There are lots of ways kids learn about 'putting up more numbers'. They will learn that no matter what else we do.

In Living My Dream, I tried to find another definition of winning. I said,

The winning and losing are different, you see

They look a bit different upon victory

The ones who have won are the ones who have played
The victors are those whose best efforts were made

We don't grow because we WIN. We grow because we COMPETE. Victory is not measured on the scoreboard, but, rather in our HEARTS.

For my part, I'll choose to teach character, confidence and team work. I'll talk about sportsmanship and fair play. I'll throw in some encouragement, caring and even some love. I have the gifts to do that. I believe it is part of my responsibility to use them.

I'll let the winning take care of itself. I'll run my race as well as I can. I'll let God choose who the winners are.

STEPPING STONES

Remember that sports are something we *play*.

How do you define 'winning?' Try writing your own definition.

Can you reward effort as often as scoring points?

Can you have the same positive attitude after a game well played as a game won?

Can you treat Triumph and Disaster the same?

Finding
the
Steps

*"You shall walk in all the way which
the Lord your God has commanded you..."*
—Deuteronomy 5[9]

Once you can see the destination of your journey, you must find the path that will take you there. Then, like the knight who got off his horse, you must be able to show your followers the steps across the water. Although we may be able to envision the destination ourselves, in order for others to follow, we must be able to describe the path to them in terms they can understand. We must be able to paint them a picture so they can share our vision. What will the path look like for them?

The Kingdom

"Where there is no vision the people perish."
—Proverbs 29[10]

It is sometimes difficult for young people to see the path to the destination. Even the games they play present challenges. Soccer is a great example. The objective of the game; the positions of the players; and the relationships that they have to each other seem complex and are often difficult for children to grasp.

When they are on the field, because of their size, their view is limited. They can only see what they are doing. Often they do not even see what is in front of them, because they have their eyes on the ball or on the player they are trying to avoid. They usually can not see what is behind them or on either side. They certainly can not see the stepping stones that will lead them to the other side of the river! So, those of us who have found the path already must help the children see where they are going.

I have found that to help children become successful at this game, three things can make a difference. First, we must find a way to let the children step back and see the whole picture rather than just the parts. What does the path look like? Secondly, we need to show them how the parts fit together. Where are the stones they can step on along the way? And thirdly, we need to help them hear and understand the terminology that comes with the new game. What shall we call these steps?

Here's an example of how I have addressed these challenges. One day I had a practice with a group of five-year-olds (micros) whose total experience with soccer was the one practice they had had the previous week with me. I was struggling with how to help them understand the concepts of the game. So, I asked myself,

"What do these kids understand? What can they relate to? How can I help them see the game in their terms and on their level?"

To help myself, I got down on my knees and looked at it from their perspective. What did it look like to them? What could they see? What could they not see? How could they relate? From down close to the ground, I found an answer. I saw a fairy tale. Young children think in terms of fairy tales. They hear them everyday. That might be a place to start. I could explain the game as a fairy tale! Surely, they would see and understand. So, I made up a tale about the Kingdom of Soccer.

At the next practice, I sat the young players down on the side of the field and I told them a tale about a Great Wizard (the league director) who oversaw a Kingdom (our league) of countries (teams like ours). Each country had its own castle (a goal) which must be protected; because inside each castle lay a marvelous treasure.

I explained that in front of each castle, positioned to protect the treasure was a special guard called a goalie. This guard had special powers. Unlike the other players, he could use his hands to touch the ball as long as he stayed inside the castle walls (in the box) Surrounding the goalie were other guards (called defenders) who stayed near the goal to help the goalie ward off oncoming troops and stop the ball. Their main job was to protect the castle.

At the other end of the field, there were knights on horseback (called forwards) who could take the ball; run to the far end and kick it in the other team's castle.

I told the players that when a team kicks the ball in the goal, they get to take part of the other team's treasure (described as precious jewels, earrings, necklaces, gold coins—plus items such as American Girls dolls and video games that were treasures in their minds). This was the reason for the knights to kick the ball in the other goal and for our guards to stop oncoming attacks.

As I told the story, the kids sat on the sidelines while I directed their moms and dads to take the positions I described. Without being involved, they were able to see the whole picture and how the pieces fit together - this was their first glimpse of the stepping stones and the path to the other side. From that moment, they began to understand the concepts of soccer because it was explained to them in terms they knew...one step at a time.

Show them the way. Show them the path in terms that they understand. The terms can be translated into real soccer terms later. The terminology was not important at this point. In the short term, whether the player calls himself a goalie or a castle guard is not important, so long as he stands in the proper position. It makes no difference if we call the forward a knight on horseback, so long as he scores goals! Eventually the terms matter, but not at this point.

As my players took the field the next time, they understood the path to our destination. Mindful of the treasure that lay behind him in the castle, the goalie stood dutifully by the goal and seldom wandered from it. The defenders understanding that they were also charged with defending our treasure, stayed in their positions, not trying to attack the other end. From the sidelines, I encouraged them to protect their treasure, not to stay in goal. They understood. Our treasure was safe!

At the other end, the forwards ran free. They could see that there were others who were protecting the treasure. They were free to attack, so, when the opportunity came, (the ball came to them) they were off trying to put the ball in the goal and take some treasure from the other team.

Through the tale of the Kingdom of Soccer, my team saw the objectives of the game. The players understood the path to their destination. When we started to play, they were initially focused on the overall team goal, rather than the individual pieces. We were immediately successful. In the weeks ahead, we would work on individual skills; but, having started this way, my team was going to remember the overall objective, no matter how their individual skills progressed.

So often, we hear of teams that have great players with great individual skills, but the team can not bring it all together. What strikes me is that this big picture approach gets everyone moving in the same direction much faster. It gets them working as a team from the beginning. Even before individuals have the chance to use their individual skills to outshine others, they must work together. The team concept is established early. The overall objectives are shared.

Look over the whole kingdom. See the big picture. See the overall goals and objectives. Protect the treasure. Protect the team. Protect each other. Don't focus on yourself. Focus on the Kingdom.

STEPPING STONES

Do your players see the path to the destination?

Have you painted them a picture so they can share your vision?

Have you helped them understand the team objectives in terms they can understand?

Do they understand how the pieces fit together?

Will You Dance?

"When you get the choice to sit it out or dance, I hope you dance."
—Lee Ann Womack[11]

As we continue on our journey, as we learn the lessons, find the stones, and see the path; we have to choose whether to go back and lead the others. Each of us can do it. The choice is up to us! Here's another of my little poems to consider while you pause to make your decision:

Each of Us Can Dribble

Each of us can dribble
Each of us can pass

Each of us can rebound
We all can run real fast

Each of us can block a kick and that is really great
Each of us plays defense on the one we call "prom date"

We all know how to play the game just to have some fun
Then, at the end, cheer about the good things we have done.

We all know that the difference is not to win or lose
Above all else the question is simply if we choose

If we choose to dance while we hold another's hand
If we choose to sing out loud with the music from the band

He said, all things are possible in Him who strengthens me
So if we try, to do ALL things, then maybe we will see

That we can do the one thing that God asked us from the start
We can reach out to each other with the LOVE that's in our heart!

STEPPING STONES

Each of us is the sum total of the decisions we have made in our lives. Will you make the decision to lead the children?

"A bridge never crossed is a life never lived"

Taking
the
Lead

"If any one would be first, he must be last of all and servant of all."
—Mark 9[12]

Many know the way. Many can describe the destination. Many can see the path and know the steps to show others. Unfortunately, only a few actually make the commitment to take others by the hand and lead them on the journey. Some take the step voluntarily, while others may find themselves leading because of other reasons.

No matter how you get there, the important thing is having the courage to stay out front and encouraging others to follow you. You must show them you care. You must earn their trust. And very often, you must be patient while others choose to follow.

Who's Going to Coach Us?

They don't care how much you know,
until they know how much you care.

I began coaching one season as an assistant coach on a U-10 soccer team. One week we had a game scheduled in the middle of the week. At the last minute, the head coach, a dentist, had an emergency and could not be at the game. He called and asked that I step in for him that evening. I was excited. My first head coaching assignment! I had been looking forward to this. I knew I could do it.

That evening the players showed up and I took them through warm-ups just like I had done before all the previous games. Things were going well as usual. As we ended the warm-ups, I called them into our circle so I could give the usual pre-game instructions. I began by telling them that Coach Scott had something come up and that he was not going to be at the game tonight. In an encouraging voice, I tried to use his absence as a rallying point, telling the players that we could go ahead without Coach, if we all pulled together and did our jobs as he had taught us. With visions of the Gipper in my mind, I told them that we needed to win this one for Coach Scott. I was pumped!

Any questions before we start, I asked. One boy's hand rose. As I acknowledged him, I anticipated a last minute question about our strategy or the need for some last minute advice about how to play. To my surprise, the little boy asked innocently, "But, WHO is going to coach us?"

My ego immediately shrunk to a place where it belonged. This little boy had asked the honest question. In his voice I could hear all the questions in his mind. Who IS going to coach us? Have you ever done this before? What makes you think you can do this as well as Coach Scott? This is OUR game. We need some one to lead us!

I thought to myself. What makes me think I can do this? I have never done it before. I have watched and learned, but is that enough? No matter what the level of coaching, I had not yet proven myself—especially to this player. This little boy knew that.

I quickly got some perspective. While this may seem to be only a recreational league soccer game between two teams of 10 year olds not having much significance in the global scheme of things; at this moment, this game was the most important thing in this player's life!

He had thought about the game all day. He had told his friends that he has playing soccer tonight. It was likely that one of the players on the other team went to his school and this game was being played for this week's bragging rights on the playground. His dad had left work early to come see him play. His thirteen-year-old sister had been dragged by his mother to watch him play. He was ready to play. He was ready to show what he had. He was ready to do his best. He was counting on every one doing their part. And now, I had said that the head coach was not there. WHO was going to take his place, anyway? This was important!

So with my line ups in hand and my ego in check, I looked at the player and said as confidently as I could, "How about if I give it a try?" He looked back at me and thought about it a moment. I could almost see him process it. I know this guy. He comes to practice. He seems to know what he is doing. He helps Coach Scott. He cares about us. He laughs and plays with us. Yeah, I think maybe he could do it. The player's expression changed to approval. He simply said "OK".

Reassured for himself and all the other players, we moved on. All hands together in the circle, our customary 'GO TEAM' and we were onto the game.

Fortunately, the game went well. I coached well enough so no one questioned what I did. All the players, including the one who asked the question, played well and we won the game. Up to now, I had been an assistant coach. No matter how good I thought I was; no matter what I thought I could do; I had not done more. I had not proven myself. It took a 10 year old boy to help me understand by asking that question,"Who is going to coach us?"

God speaks to us in many ways through many people. On that day, he helped me understand my place through the question of a little boy. That experience taught me an important lesson. Kids do not take you at your word. If you want them to understand, you truly do have to SHOW them. Until I SHOWED this little boy that I could coach a game, he did not believe that I could. And, he had no reason to believe it. But, once I showed him I could do it, he was willing to follow me again and again. They do not always hear what you say, but they always see what you do.

Sometimes it is difficult. However, sometimes it is as easy as asking kids to give you a chance and, then, giving it your best effort.

What would you expect from your leader? Don't expect your players' trust and respect. You must earn it. You must get down on their level; play with them; show them that you care; show them you can do it. Get off your horse. Take them by the hand. They may follow you forever.

STEPPING STONES

I start every practice with a simple question: "What happened (in your life) since last practice?" Or, "How have you been?" This translates to:"I care about you as a person, not just a soccer player".

In practice I often demonstrate a new drill myself. Sometimes the best thing I can do is to make a mistake the first time. My players know that I am not perfect! But, they appreciate my efforts!

What have you done to show your players that you care?

One Fish at a Time

"Follow Me and I will make you become fishers of men."
—Mark 1[13]

We can not all change the world. Maybe no one person can change the world. But with faith, I believe we can each change a small part of it. Every season that I coach, I have the opportunity to change a bit of the world—made up of eight to sixteen kids. Sometimes I am able to make a small impact on all of them. Sometimes I reach one or two. Certainly, there have been seasons when I do not reach any of the kids. But I try. I continue to try year after year after year.

Robbie Moore, a former pastor and good friend of mine once told me that as followers of Jesus, our job is to fish for disciples to bring to Christ. But he was quick to add that our job was not to catch those disciples. He believed that our job was just to locate them and throw them a line. Whether they bite (and come to Christ) or not is a matter between them and God. In other words, it is God's job to reel them in.

Robbie said that just like fishing, we should only focus on one fish at a time. When we fish, we do not expect to pull in many at once. Think about it. Throw the line, get a bite, hook a fish and pull it in. You are delighted with your success. You are not disappointed that two or three more fish did not jump on the line. So, it is with helping kids find Jesus. Throw the line to all. See who bites. If you get one bite, be satisfied. If the time is right, God will reel him in.

Then, you try again. Just like fishing, it often takes many casts and much patience to land the first one. Ask any fisherman. Even landing one good one can be enough to call it a successful day. With one fish on your stringer, you can go home pleased with yourself, your efforts, your strategy and your results. You will have a story to tell. And, catching that one will be enough to make you come back for more.

Look to the soccer field. Bait the hooks. Throw out the lines. Cast out the devotionals. Walk like Christ. Hope that someone bites. When they do, handle them carefully. Talk to them. Take them by the hand. Show them the way. Then, let God do the rest. He will. He told us he will. Bring them close to the boat; God will help them get in with us.

Several years ago I was coaching my son's U-12 soccer team. It was a good team full of fifth, sixth and a few seventh graders. At the end of one practice, I planned to present a devotional based on the story of David and Goliath. Before I began, I asked if anyone would like to tell the popular story for us. To my surprise and delight, a seventh grade boy named Drew raised his hand and volunteered. He gave a wonderful account of the story complete with analysis and lessons to be learned. He emphasized that rather than using the armor and weapons he had been offered by the others, David had used the weapons he knew best to defeat the bigger and stronger Goliath.

I could not have been more pleased. My player had told the story and made the point I had hoped to reveal. I was feeling great. Perhaps this coaching thing was coming together for me after all!

I had learned that whenever possible, using a visual aid would help the players remember the lesson. This day, I had come prepared. I had collected a bag of small smooth stones like the ones David must have used. At the end of Drew's recitation, I placed one pebble in the hand of each player. I suggested that the stone could be a reminder of the story. Like David, I suggested they use their own special gifts in the upcoming game that Saturday. I suggested that the players might even bring the pebbles to the game to remind them of their gifts and as a kind of good luck charm. Each player clutched the pebble in the palm of his hand, as we bowed our heads and prayed to close the practice.

As always, I went to work on my after practice routine of gathering balls, pinnies and cones; and listening to comments and questions from the parents. As the last ones on the field, I walked to the parking lot with my son. I was feeling particularly good, because I felt I had hit a home run with the devotional that day. Player participation; all the players seemed to be interested; and they left with a reminder of the lesson. All just as I had hoped.

However, my balloon quickly deflated when my son confided in me that after I had turned away, several of the boys had thrown their stones at the headstones in the cemetery that was adjacent to our practice field. Boys will be boys! Give them a projectile and target practice is bound to follow. I should have known. I tried to push it off and not show my disappointment to my son, but I was dejected as we drove home.

Throughout the week, the thought of the boys wasting their stones on target practice stayed on my mind. I was alternatively sad and mad and then frustrated about what I could have done differently. The thoughts wore on me all week, even up to game time that Saturday. Then the Lord spoke to me clearly.

As one of my youngest and smallest players ran onto the field to greet me that day, he held out his hand with his palm wide open and the pebble laying on it. He looked at me and said, "I've got my stone, Coach!" He closed it in his hand and ran onto the field to join the others in warm-ups. He held onto that pebble throughout the rest of the game; and as I remember, we won the contest.

The words of Robbie Moore came back to me. Fish! One at a time! Patience! Let the Lord do His work!

That week I learned my lesson. Throw out the lines. If you catch just one, be happy with your success. Move on. Let God do His work in His time. If they do not bite: if they do not follow; just like a good fisherman, BE PATIENT. Let the lines lie. In time, some will find them and the hungry ones will come to be fed.

Every season now, I fish for disciples. But, I have learned my lesson. I fish for one at a time.

STEPPING STONES

Give the players something to remind them of the lessons you
teach them on the field.

Be patient - be satisfied with small successes when appropriate.
Remember your role. You are not working alone.

Run 'em and Love 'em

Each journey begins with a single step.
—Chinese Proverb

Because I have coached so many teams, other coaches often ask for my advice. I guess they figure they have seen me around for so long, I must know something. I am always willing to share because so many others have shared with me.

One year, one of my friends who had been my assistant coach for a number of seasons decided to step up to his first head coaching position. He volunteered to be the coach of his daughter's micro soccer team. He came to me and said, "Coach, how do I get started?"

We sat and had a long talk. We reviewed the philosophy of the league and the approach he had seen me follow with teams before when I had coached both of his older sons. I even prepared a practice plan for him. It detailed drills which I had used successfully over the years. Each was carefully diagramed and I took the time to explain how to run each one. When he asked how to get these kindergarteners and first graders to understand the game, I told him the story about the Kingdom of Soccer.

When I had finished, he seemed satisfied that I had given him what he needed. However, he still seemed a bit overwhelmed with it all. I could see that he was wondering, "How can I remember all this?" "How can I make this all work?" "How can I pull together a crisp practice like I have seen other coaches do?"

Seeing his concern, I finished by saying simply, "Jim, if all else fails, just run 'em and love 'em". He smiled and nodded. From those words, he understood, that all I had done over the years could be summed up that briefly, "Run 'em and love 'em." After all, that is what we are all about. Show the players that someone cares and let them have fun. How bad could that be? In the end it will all be alright. Show them you love them. Let them play.

Run 'em and love 'em! Indeed.

STEPPING STONES

The greatest gift I have given my players is my love.

Too often we try to make things too complicated. Keep it simple.

Think back to the goals you (and your players) set at the beginning of the season. Was one of the first ones,"Have Fun?"

Don't lose that perspective.

Knowing
Your
Followers

I am the good shepherd;
I know my own and my own know me.
—John 10[14]

Once you have found the path for yourself, and you have stepped to the front, you must identify who you want to lead. The better you know them, the easier it will be to lead them as they take the steps with you.

Ask yourself, "Who have I chosen to lead? Who will follow me? Do I know who they are? What are their names? What will I call them? Do I understand all their individual gifts?

How will you get to know them? Will they answer your call? Do you know how you will bring all the individuals together as one team? How can you make all the pieces of your puzzle fit together? Can you get all your players to know each other? To work together? To encourage each other? To love each?

I believe you can.

What Did You Call Me?

Emi Ush, Hanner Bananer, and the Drama Queen

Who are these guys? At the beginning of the first practice of each season, I gather my players in a tight circle. I talk to them about the goals for the season. I tell them that the most important goals are to have fun, make friends and support each other. I tell them how important it is to love one another. In order to do that, I tell them we must get to know each other. We must know each other's names. I tell them, I will not tolerate players saying things like "Hey you, pass it to me"; or, "Get it to the tall kid, he's open".

I tell them we must learn each other's names. I tell them we must learn the thing that makes each of us unique. I say doing that will help make us friends.

So, around the circle we go, each player saying his name and something else about himself. Depending on the age and season they tell where they go to school, their favorite music, favorite flavor of ice cream or what they want for Christmas. By doing this, we begin the process of knowing each other. Soon we will go the next step and find out who has a good shot, where they like to shoot from, who can play defense, who is fast and who can play goalie. For now, the names are enough.

I love communication. I love building relationships. I want to talk to my players often—some say, constantly, both in practice and in games. I cheer, I direct, I encourage. I like to call players by their names. So, in order to get out instructions and names quickly, I like to use short hand ...names I can blurt out in an instant...names that will not be mistaken for someone else. Have you had as many Emilys and Samanthas on your teams as I have had on mine? And, how quickly can you say "Mary Elizabeth"?

With this objective in mind, now, as I go around that circle at the first practice, I also ask for a "nickname". I ask, "What would you like me to call you from the sideline? For whom would you like us to cheer?" Many have an answer ready. Emily is "Emi", Samantha is "Sammie". Where two have the same name, we work it out. Emily Usher has been "Emi Ush" for years to distinguish her from "Emi G" and "Emi D".

I have been amused by some of the nicknames that the players tell me, often despite their parents' wishes. A favorite player named Caroline wanted to be called "Carrie", even though her mother disliked that shortened version of her given name. I did not know about her mother's feelings, so I innocently accepted it as her nickname for the season. For twelve-year-old Caroline, perhaps it was another step towards independence. At the same time, that name gave her a special bond with her teammates and coach, because no one else used that name. By the way, what could her mother say on game day when her teammates cheered so enthusiastically for "Carrie"?

So many times, these players reveal something inside, when they tell you their names. A name says something special about them. It's as if they take down their guard for a moment and let you behind that mask the real world requires them to hide behind. Knowing these names helps me understand the players and move closer to their hearts.

Once an eleven-year-old proudly revealed her nickname to be D.Q., short for "The Drama Queen!" As the season progressed, I learned that her name said a lot about her personality! There was never a dull moment when she was around!

On a high school basketball team, one player affectionately referred to his 6'3", 240 pound teammate as Biscuit—because he said he could not pass by even one biscuit without eating it. Accepting the name with the love it was given, we called him Biscuit the rest of the season.

When players have no nicknames for themselves, I usually come up with one. It's something I like to do. A toothless first grader named Hannah will for always be known to me as 'Hanner Bananer'. A micro player who loved to play defense is known to me as Iron Will. And because of me, a cute little girl with a mouthful of name—Annazelle—is known throughout our league as A.Z.

Knowing each other's names helps players become friends quicker and easier. I have found that players who are friends play better together. Players who are friends will give and go—sharing opportunities to score. Friends protect each others' backsides on defense when they rotate on defense. Friends help each other. Friends encourage each other. Friends work together. Friends play better.

When players become your friends, they become loyal to you. The will do things for you on the field that they will not do for others. They try harder. They try new things. They work with other players. The results improve. When you take care of your players, the winning will take care of itself.

I reinforce this concept during warm-ups at each practice and before each game also. While I could simply stand aside and allow my players to run the drills themselves or allow my assistants to lead them; I like to be right in the middle of it all. I lead the drills. I am the one who passes the ball to each player as he goes for the goal and takes a shot. I am the one who makes the initial pass before they give and go. I am the one who takes a shot at each defender before they make the stop.

With each pass and each shot, I am talking to that individual player. I say everything from "I know you're gonna have a great game" to "Nice shot" to "How was that chemistry test yesterday?" to just, "Ain't it a great day?" That brief personal connection shows once again that I care about these kids as people, not just players. It shows that I know more about them than what position they play. With the whole team listening, it shows that I care about them all. I care about them. They care about me. We all care about each other.

One of my rewards is that many of these kids remain my friends. After they have outgrown the league, some come back to the fields to watch and encourage the younger players. Many even come back from college. They stand on the sidelines and continue to share their dreams for the future. My friendships have led me to write recommendation letters for college and job applications. In the spring, we often see prom pictures of former ten-year-old defenders who have blossomed into beautiful young women. Someday, I am hoping for a wedding invitation from one of my oldest players. What better gift can we give than to be a friend?

For years around our league, I have been known simply as Coach Jeff. Many who greet me on the field do not know my last name and never will. Yet, nothing says more about who I am or who I want to be than that nickname!

Our names are important to us. What people call us is even more important. If you want someone to follow, you need to understand who they are. Their nickname may give you a glimpse into their soul. If nothing else, it can give you a special connection that few others will have. Either way, it will be easier for you to lead and for them to follow.

STEPPING STONES

At the first practice I come with name tags for each player, so all will get to know each others' names right away.

At the second practice, I revise the name tags to show the nicknames we have discovered.

Do you have a nickname that the players call you? What does that name say about you?

We Are All One Body

How can the drops of water know themselves to be a river?
—Zen Saying

After we have been introduced as individuals, we need to find how we fit together as a team. We need to learn about the importance of the team over the individuals. I like to take this next step with the help of a scripture lesson. I use 1 Corinthians, which says "For just as we have many members in one body, and all the members do not have the same function, so we who are many are one body in Christ and individually members one of another".

In his letter, the Apostle Paul makes some important points about how the team concept should work in our lives. This is one of the lessons I believe we need to pass on.

First, Paul says that each of us has been given gifts according to the grace of God. None of us should think more of ourselves than others, because each of us is only as good as God allows us to be.

Secondly, Paul tells us we all have our own gifts. He says each of us is important. Each has something to contribute. We all should value each other.

Thirdly, and most importantly, Paul talks about how all our gifts come together. He compares the members of the church to members of a body. He talks about how all the parts of the body have different functions, but how they are all dependent upon each other. For example, the lesson says, that if the head has no legs to stand on, it will go nowhere. All the parts support each other.

With this lesson in mind, I have made comparisons to the players on a soccer team. All the players have unique gifts and talents. All the players have value. None of the players can be successful (stand) alone. But when they support each other, they can accomplish great things.

A visual aid has helped me explain this concept especially with the younger players. First, I show them a diagram of the field with all the players (Xs) in proper position.

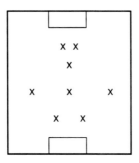

Using this diagram, I talk about how the players are positioned and how they all need to stay in their places, maintain spacing and do their assigned jobs.

After this coaching moment, I ask the players if they know what a constellation is. They usually tell me that it is a group of stars in the sky. They tell me if you look at it just right you can see a picture. They describe for me a big dipper or a bear or a hunter. Right! A constellation is a group of stars, if you look at them individually; or it can be a picture of something bigger and better if you look at it with a broader point of view.

Back to the diagram. Is this a group of individual stars? Let's look at it through different eyes. Suppose we connect the dots, like we do with a constellation. What do we get? I connect the dots to make them form a "stick man"—usually with a "happy face".

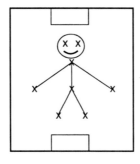

With the dots connected, we can see ONE player with many different parts. Some are the eyes, the nose, the head; some are the hands, some are the feet. Just like Paul said. Together we are one body. Together we support each other.

A picture is worth a thousand words. With the constellation in hand, I tell the players, "Let's start looking at each other this way. Not as individual stars, but as one body. One body that functions together. One body that suffers together. One body that will rejoice together. No longer many individual players, but one team!" With the help of an old letter from some guy named Paul and a little astronomy, the team building process begins.

I came up with this idea while walking on the beach with my wife one summer day. As I drew soccer plays in the sand with a stick, I suddenly saw the bigger picture. Connecting those dots, I found my first constellation. You never know when inspiration will come! Look up in the sky at the stars and the clouds. Look down at the sand on the beach. Look! Then, look again! Look! You may find something that God wants you to see!

STEPPING STONES

Some coaches give each of their players a piece of a jigsaw puzzle to explain the same concept of many pieces fitting together to make a bigger picture.

I see teaching tools every day. The constellation was one. Look in common places for uncommon signs.

Honk! Honk!

"Make a joyful noise unto the Lord..."
—Psalm 100[15]

Whenever we see geese flying overhead, they are in a "V" formation. Our attention is drawn to them by the familiar honking they make as they fly together.

I have been told that geese can fly some 70% farther when in formation than they can by themselves. The formation cuts the wind for those in the back. And, they alternate as the leader, each taking his turn cutting the wind.

And the honking? I have been told that if the lead goose were to turn his head and look back to check on his followers, the force of the wind would break his long fragile neck. So, the others honk constantly to let the leader know they are still there. Then, he doesn't need to look back.

What a great teaching example for my players. Would we play 70% better if we stayed in formation and played together? What if we alternated being the leader? Everybody could take a turn. Everyone is a leader. We are stronger as a team. These are important concepts drawn from an everyday example. I like that.

The part I like the best is the honking! Constant noise from the followers to let the leader know they are still there. "We are still behind you" "Don't worry, we won't leave you" "Keep up the good work" "We've got your backside". This is encouragement in its simplest form.

I have often used this lesson. One game day I took it a step further. After telling the goose story during practice; I wrote "HONK!! HONK!!" with my sharpie on the back of my coaches' shirts and wore it to the next game. As we warmed up, I showed my U-11 girls the words on my back. I told them as we played today; I wanted all of the players on the sidelines to make constant noises of encouragement to those on the field. As we finished and gathered for our team cheer, all hands in, that day we all made a loud HONK! HONK!

At the prayer circle, I explained to the parents gathered there what we had been doing and showed them the writing on my shirt. I asked that they join us in encouragement as we played that day.

The game began and I strode up and down the sidelines as usual—this day with the words HONK! HONK!—staring the fans in the face. As I walked in front of them, some were brave enough to go along and begin loud honking. Others were at least encouraged to cheer louder and more often than usual! Another lesson learned! We are all stronger together than alone. How about if we fly together from now on?

Another season, I had a team called Team Spain. With the help of my son and a Spanish-English dictionary, I found the word divertirse. It means "Let's have fun". I wrote the word on the back of another old shirt. (I have plenty of old shirts!) That day, all over the soccer complex, I got lots of questions about the meaning of the word. When I responded, it means "Let's have fun!" I got smiles and approving looks. I could see the thoughts, "Hey, Coach Jeff is going to have fun today, why don't we?" A simple reminder. A little nudge in the right direction.

When you see geese flying, do you hear their words of encouragement?

STEPPING STONES

Be a living example of the lessons you are teaching.

Find something to write on the back of your shirt and wait for the reaction. One day I taped a sign on my back that said:

> Today is my day to have fun!
> How 'bout you?

With Individual Gifts

After instilling the team concept and the necessity of working together, I find it equally important to teach 'balance'. Each player must also appreciate the importance of his individual contributions—no matter what they may be. My responsibility is to identify those individual gifts; then, help the players see and develop them.

I go back to the lessons of St. Paul where we learned about our individual gifts and talents and how all our gifts contributed to one body. I emphasize the point that we all have gifts and that we need to use them to the greatest extent possible. By doing so, collectively we will be a better team.

As I discover the gifts of each player, I encourage their development. I encourage those with scoring ability to take the shot. I encourage those with ball handling and passing ability to find the open man and those gifted defensive players to make the stop. Often others are encouraged to be the leaders, to help the younger players, or to help keep us focused.

I found a great way to encourage and reward the individual contributions while balancing the needs of the team. It is my lollipop ritual at the end of the game. During the course of each game, I keep statistics on the contributions of each player. Different than traditional "stats", in addition to goals and saves, my statistics include items like hustle, effort and attitude. Truly, I try to keep track of all the things that have helped us to play well that day.

For some players, the stats are easy. Goals scored. Assists made. Saves made. For others, they are more difficult to capture. Midfielders maintaining their positions and spacing. Players moving the ball to others in scoring position. Outstanding effort (measured by what that player has to give.) Encouragement of teammates ("honking" from the bench!) usually shows up on my sheet. The point is to find something positive that each player has contributed to the team in every game.

When the game is over, I gather all the players in a circle where they can see me and each other. I go down the roster and point out the contributions of each player. I show as much enthusiasm for the first player as the last and as much for the strongest player as the weakest. As I recognize each player, I hand him a lollipop. I ask the parents and other fans to celebrate along with us. Each player gets a hearty round of applause.

At the end when everyone has been recognized and has his sucker in hand, the players and fans can see that each player did make a contribution "according to his gifts and talents".

Early in the season everyone begins to realize that all the contributions do make a difference. Spontaneously, during the rest of the games, they begin to cheer for all the subtle efforts (e.g., position, support) as loudly as they used to cheer for the more obvious ones (e.g., goals and saves).

Often at the first game of the season, after all the suckers have been distributed and the accolades expressed, I like to say in a dry tone, "I wanted to recognize those players who made a difference for the team today. I have only recognized those who truly made a difference for us. I gave lollipops to those players. So, if you are one of those who received a pop, I need you to make sure to come back next week to help us again." Then I say, "Will all those players who got a sucker, hold it up so we can see who you are?"

By now, the younger players have lost track. They were so proud to have gotten their own sucker; they have not seen that everyone has one. So, they proudly thrust their lollipops up in the air. In a moment, they realize that EVERYONE has a sucker held high in his hand. Last season, one young girl with blonde pigtails exclaimed, "We ALL got one!" Smiles all around. Point made!! The learning has begun!

Now this may seem like a silly little exercise that works for a game or so and then loses its impact. That is what I thought when I started this ritual years ago. But after some 40 seasons with players ranging from 5 to 18, to my amazement, it still works!

In a recent season, I was leading a boys' high school basketball team with young men as old as eighteen and as tall as 6' 4". For the first time I questioned how my lollipops might be received. So, as I took out my bag after the first game, I said somewhat apologetically, "Now some of you may think what I am about to do is a bit silly, but it is important to me." But, before I could go further, almost on cue, my oldest player and the high scorer for the game, chipped in, "What do you mean, coach? This is my favorite part of the game!" Nothing but positive reaction after that. Each player listened to his accomplishments and willingly accepted his reward. My wife has often reported seeing these big boys driving away from our games in their own cars with suckers hanging out of their mouths. Chalk one up for being corny and straight forward!

Why are these lollipops so important? We ALL like recognition for our accomplishments and this is a way to praise everyone all the time. Some of these little people play hard and work their back sides off each week; but without scoring goals, their efforts would never show in the box score statistics. I have found my way to give them credit for that effort.

What about the advantage for the team? I have learned this. In a team sport like soccer, many players feel they get lost in the crowd. It is easy for players to think no one cares how they play among all the other players on the field. Not on my teams. From the moment they are handed their first lollipop, my players know that I am watching them the whole game. How else could I remember the nice throw-in they made in the second quarter or the stop they made on the far side of the field just before halftime? They think coach sees it all. Coach is always watching me.

When they know someone is watching for all the good things they could do, they make those things happen. They play harder and better. They all raise the level of their play because they know they will be rewarded for it. By doing so, the level of the team play is raised. Success comes more often. How do you make the team better, you ask? Play better yourself! Play so you will earn your candy! Sometimes it sounds so easy!

By the way, this is not as easy as it sounds. In the heat of a game, it is not easy to remember all those little things I want to talk about at the end of the game. So, I carry my stat sheet with me throughout the game and scribble notes all the time. By the end of the game, I have all I need.

You may ask, doesn't this take away from my focus on the overall strategy of winning the game? Sure it does! But I have committed myself to doing more than winning games. I want to build confidence and team work. Personally, keeping the list makes me focus on what is important. I focus on each player's efforts and development, then, I recognize and reward them. Over the years I have discovered that if I take care of the players, they will take care of the winning!

As a devotional, I have asked my players, what might happen if we all walked around with a bag of lollipops like the one I have. I have wondered with them, what would happen if we all gave out lollipops all the time? What if, when someone gave their best effort, we said "good job" and handed them a sucker? What if, when someone was nice to us, we said, "Thank you" and gave them a lollipop? What if, when someone was sad, we just reached in our bag, pulled out a lollipop and said, "I care"? What if...

Do you suppose they give out candy after every game in Heaven?

STEPPING STONES

I use a chart like this to keep my statistics for each player:

Team Iceland					
	1st	2nd	3rd	4th	Comments
Caroline	Goal		Good free kick		
Luis		Great header		Effort	Best individual effort of the season
Maria		Great Position		Takeaway	
Yvette	Assist to Caroline		Pass to Anna		Came back from sprained ankle
Anna	Throw in	Block		Assist to Zach	
Andres	Leadership		Goal		
Kenny		2 saves	Assist to Andres	Cheering for Luis	
Kelly		Strong defense		Takeaway	
Megan	Smart play		Talking to others		
Zach				Goal	

Taking
the
Steps

"...if you have faith as a grain of mustard seed, you will say to this mountain, 'Move hence to yonder place,' and it will move."
—Matthew 17[17]

Although someone showed each of us the steps the first time, as we attempt to lead others, we must be able to find the steps by ourselves—again and again. As time goes on, we all find that there are many steps. There are different paths to reach each destination. Each path is good, if it leads you to your dream. Ideally, we must find the steps that are best suited to our own gifts.

From time to time, you may take a different path because of many reasons. At times you may find that the path itself has changed. Sometimes different stepping stones appear in the water because the current in the river shifts. However, if you stay committed, you will find the steps. And, no matter which path you choose, there will always be others to help you find the stones and keep your balance.

By now you have made a commitment, you have seen your destination and others are beginning to follow. From here you must go forward BOLDLY. You must take the steps. Take the ones that you can find. Take them one at a time. Move forward with confidence.

A Game by
Any Other Name

Start where you are
Use what you have
Do what you can

Give it a try. Often I have heard a well-intended parent say, "I would like to coach, but I don't know anything about the game. Jeff, you know so much about the game, how could I ever measure up to you and the others?"

My answer is simple. First, put your role in perspective. As coaches of children, our job is not so much to make better soccer players, as it is to make better people. It is not so much that we win games, but that we build relationships among players, between coaches and players, and between young people and God. If you are willing to pursue those goals, you can learn the game.

I am a great example that most anyone can be successful leading kids. When I started as a soccer coach, I knew next to nothing about the game, but I learned. If I can do it, so can you! Remember, God only gives us what we can handle!

I grew up in the seventies in Indiana. We had three, maybe four sports that most kids played—football, basketball, baseball and hockey. Smack in the middle of Hoosier Hysteria, everyone played basketball at some level. Personally, I was intrigued by ice hockey.

When I was approached to coach soccer, I thought the same as everyone else. I have never played the game. (Well, maybe once in junior high gym class!) I had never read a book about soccer and I had never even seen a game played in person. So what should I do?

I thought to myself, use what you already know. Go with your instincts. So, I thought about what I knew. I knew about hockey. Take a puck, put it in a goal. Team work, spacing, passing, and shooting—that all made sense to me. Is soccer all that different when we substitute a ball on grass? In hockey, there are designated offensive and defensive players. Players play their positions. Players must keep proximity between themselves. All the players try to protect their own goal.

There is even "offsides" in both games. Offsides is different in soccer, but, I understood the concept. It is a bit more complicated in soccer, but not really. If I understood that much, I figured I could learn the rest.

In basketball, a sport I know and love, the concepts are also similar to soccer. There are two teams playing between a set of lines trying to put a ball in a goal. There are rules like not walking, no double dribbling, etc. But there are rules in soccer, too—like not using your hands. As I have learned more, I now often describe soccer as basketball on the ground!

Give and go—that is a fundamental in all these sports. Fast breaks also look alike—move the ball to the middle, players fill their lanes, pass to the open man, and every one go to the goal for the rebound—the more I thought, the more these sports looked alike to me.

Try to find the match ups that benefit you the most. Go one-on-one when you can. Shoot when you're open. All the players wear short pants. Soccer and basketball didn't seem that different.

When I relaxed, I realized, I knew the basic concepts. I knew spacing and positions. I knew passing. I knew shooting. I knew how to "give and go". So, I decided to put them to use. How wrong could I be anyway? I gave it a try.

Before he approached Goliath, David refused his brother's armor, saying, "I can not go with these; for I have not used them". Instead, he chose his own sling and pebbles he had used before... and the rest is history. We each have our own pebbles—experiences and gifts that have worked before. Use those pebbles as your stepping stones.

STEPPING STONES

Soccer is just like basketball on the ground.

Give it a try! God only gives us what we can handle!

What do you already know about other sports or activities?

How can you apply what you already know to soccer?

The Game is
the Best Teacher

*When the work of the perfect leader is done well,
the people think they have done it all by themselves.*

—Chinese Proverb

All of us who have coached youth sports over the years have our own methods of teaching the game. Some stress the fundamentals running drill after drill after drill. Some stress conditioning using exercises, running lines and wind sprints. Others work on specific plays and game strategies.

There are as many coaching methods as there are coaches. My personal approach was encouraged by a former professional soccer coach. In a presentation during a coaching clinic, he told a group of us that drills teaching skills are important, but "the game is still the best teacher." His point was this. Let the kids play as much as you can. He said that when given the opportunity, the players will use the game to find ways to be successful and improve.

I realized that this idea fit my personality. The game can be the best teacher. I thought back to how I had learned to play most sports. When I was young, we did not have the number and variety of organized sports that we have today. Although we played the traditional sports of football, basketball and baseball in organized leagues, much of the time we spent playing sports was on our own. We played in our backyards and on the vacant lot at the end of the street.

How did we learn? We watched others and then tried to imitate them. When we were young, we watched the high school players at the football game on Friday night and then played our own game on Saturday afternoon. How many times did we watch the NBA on television on Sunday afternoon, and then run out to the driveway during halftime to try to make the moves that the pros made in the first half? We figured it out for ourselves.

I apply this same process on the soccer field. In practice I let the kids play. I let them figure it out. They seem to learn better and remember it longer if they do it themselves. As a coach, my job is to move the process along.

I try to allow as much scrimmage time as possible. I allow the kids to play. After all, ours is a recreational league. The kids are here to have fun. We practice only once each week. If we spend all our time on fundamentals and conditioning, there will be no time to play. Play. Have fun. Isn't that why we are here? Even in practice?

In my practices, I run a few drills which both get the players warmed up and work on necessary skills. But, as quickly as possible, I move to scrimmages. Here's my view. First, the kids want to play as much as possible. So, I let them play and have fun. Second, when they scrimmage for long periods during practice it works on conditioning just as effectively as running sprints at the end of practice. So, I prefer to keep my players moving in a scrimmage for as much of the practice as possible. I have found that this does work. Moving constantly for an hour and fifteen minutes challenges even the best conditioned teenager! By the second half of the season, my teams always seem to have more stamina late in the game than those who practice otherwise.

How do I allow the game to be the teacher? Here's my idea. The concept is easier to explain using basketball as an example. So, please allow me a divergence to another sport.

For the first ten minutes or so of each scrimmage, I just let them play. Let them get their energy out. These kids have been in school all day and doing homework before practice. They need a release. I let them be undisciplined and selfish. After a short while, they are a bit winded and they are ready to listen, so I proceed to teach.

Basketball requires team work. I believe in working the ball inside. I believe in getting the best shot available - which means shooting in the paint. Since the game is the best teacher, I use the game. Reminding the players that we should work the ball inside,

I simply say, "For the next ten minutes, no shots may be taken outside the paint!" Any shot taken outside the paint is a turnover.

In the first practice or so, players moan. I hear, "What no outside shots? I am a great three point shooter. How can we win without any outside shooting? Let me show you my shot. I've been practicing at home. Come on, coach."

Reluctantly, they consent and the scrimmage begins. They struggle at first. They can't get the ball inside. They think they can't score. They complain some more. In frustration a player takes a shot from the top of the key. Swish! He scores just like he has done so many times in his driveway. Other players cheer. Way to go! I blow the whistle and calmly say, "No shot, no points." "That was outside the paint. Ball to the other side."

Now, these young boys want to win. They are competitive. They do not want to give up points or give up the ball. "OK, if that's the way you want it coach, let's try again." They try again. They work hard. Some one breaks free in the lane, the point guard hits him with a pass, he makes the lay up. Two points. Coach doesn't take these away. They were in the paint! They count!

The other team gets the ball. "Come on, we're down by two. We can do that, too. Let's see, what did he do? Oh yeah … guy gets open in the middle, pass it to him, he makes a lay up." The other team tries to duplicate the efforts of the first squad. It doesn't take long. They find a way to score. Both teams begin to find their ways into the paint and scoring. I get a few looks of understanding that say, "Hey, this can work, coach."

All the time I am talking to them encouraging them and subtly giving them ideas about how to make this work. "Look for a pick! Break to the basket. Look inside!" They hear, they execute.

Periodically after a particularly effective play, I will blow the whistle for a "coaching moment". While they get a blow, I review what just happened. I explain why it worked. If need be, I walk the players through the play again, so that everyone can see what happened. I congratulate the players who ran the play. Well done! Let's all try to do that next time. They get the picture. Young eyes see the road map. The seed is planted for them to try. Believe it or not, sooner or later they try that same play themselves … and it works.

Shortly, the team begins to function as a unit. They move. They pass. They work together to get the ball inside. They begin to feel successful. They begin to believe that the coach might really know something.

Now step two. The successful plays begin to repeat and the defense gets wise. They've seen that before. They know what is coming. The play bogs down. The play gets a little ragged. They need something to move the offense a bit. They need players to move to open spaces. They need to move without the ball. They need others to pass. They need to dribble less. This is where I can be the coach.

The game is the best teacher. Don't stop the scrimmage. Don't stop the play. Don't stop the competition. Don't stop the FUN! Instead, insert some coaching. How do you get teenage boys to stop dribbling and pass? Simple. Take away the dribble. I make a rule! I am the coach; I can do what I want! I announce a new rule. "You can only dribble one time, and then you have to pass. I don't care what else you do. Just one dribble, OK? By the way, for those of you who want to dribble once and shoot from the parking lot, we still have that rule about no shots outside the paint! OK? Play on!"

You can anticipate what happens. Players without the ball begin to move around. They have to move to open spaces to get a pass from their teammate who can not dribble to them. They have to move towards the ball. They have to find ways to advance the ball towards the basket without dribbling it there. They still have to shoot in the darn paint!

As before, in the beginning there are moans and groans. In the beginning there are non-believers. But, again, someone finds a way. Someone moves. Someone cuts. Give and go! They realize that this can work. More experimenting. More coaching moments at strategic times (when they are getting tired or frustrated). Always encouraging words while they play. Most importantly, they are learning by themselves. And they are playing and having fun!

I have done this with additional limitations as well. I am a big fan of the bounce pass—especially when passing the ball inside. The last iteration usually involves shots only in the paint; only one dribble per player; and only bounce passes allowed. Anything else is a turnover. I have made up other limitations to teach skills and get results, but this sequence is my favorite.

On the soccer field, I find the same approach works for me. For example, the first step is to allow only one touch before the player must pass the ball. Then, I put limits on where shots may be taken. And, then I require that shots may only be taken with the left foot. The list of limits goes on. What's great is that the same rules make it fair for both sides; and the competition and fun never stop. There are as many variations as there are concepts to be taught. Use your imagination!

I try to plan my practices so that at the end there is time to let them play without any limitations again—just for ten minutes or so. The players feel relieved and rewarded. But it is surprising that after a full practice working with the limitations, they often continue. They have become second nature. The players come to realize that they will be more successful working together. By the way, they figured it out themselves and they had fun doing it!

As coach, sometimes I am just there to keep things organized. You see, the GAME really is the best teacher!

STEPPING STONES

To achieve my objectives for teaching specific skill development, I have tried the following:

• Restricting players to one touch before passing to another player

• Allowing players to shoot only with their left (or "off") foot

• Placing a bench in the goal to encourage shooting high or for the corners

• Allowing shots only outside the box (to work on longer shots)

Prince Ali

"...I speak to them in parables because seeing they do not see, and hearing they do not hear, nor do they understand."
—Matthew 13[18]

For those who have never played the game before, a soccer throw-in is not an easy skill to learn. As Americans, we throw baseballs and footballs with one hand; over one shoulder or even side armed. A soccer throw is different. For many, it is an awkward motion.

How do you teach this skill? Try it with a group of fourteen-year-olds. Explain how to do it. Show them how. Watch them fail the first time. It can be challenging for anyone.

To raise the degree of difficulty level, one season I needed to teach a bunch of five-year-old micro players how to do this before their first game. I knew it would be hard, so I looked for a teaching tool. Where had I seen that motion before? Could I find a frame of reference for that distinctive motion? I looked. I thought. I called upon my memory of things my daughter knew. Games, movies, videos...I thought it must be in there somewhere. Then it came to me. I found the answer in another fairy tale. This time it was an age old story—Aladdin.

At the next practice, I asked my micros, "Who has seen the movie, Aladdin?" Everyone raised their hand. Half of them spontaneously began telling me about their favorite part ... I interrupted and went on. "Do you remember when Prince Ali rode into the town on his elephant in the big parade?" Heads nodded, everyone remembered. I continued, "Do you remember how the townspeople went like this and bowed down to the Prince?"

I reminded them by making the motion myself. I started with both arms outstretched toward the sky; then bringing them behind my head and coming forward together all the way to my knees. Both arms remained straight the whole way. I waved my arms repeatedly as the townspeople had done. As I made the motion, I chanted the name of the Prince, just like in the movie. "Prince Ali, Prince Ali … Do you remember that part?" I asked. Sure, we all do. They began imitating me almost immediately from where they sat—little arms waving forward and back.

"Good. Now let's try something. Everyone line up on the sideline." They all scurried quickly to take a place on the chalk along the edge of the field facing me. I instructed them to pretend the Prince was coming and asked them to bow to him along with me. They all joined in. They were all standing on the sideline waving their arms and chanting at the imaginary Prince going by, "Prince Ali, Prince Ali." Good motion. I thought this might work!

"Now, everybody get a ball. Get back on the line. Hold the ball tightly with both hands and don't let go. Let's repeat what we just did." "Prince Ali, Prince Ali". Again, arms waving together. The ball moved from behind their heads forward to their knees. Arms together while their feet stayed planted firmly on the ground behind the sideline. So far, so good. Nice form, nice motion. We were almost there.

Now, one last step. "Hold the ball behind your head. As I say, Prince Ali, make the same motion, but this time, let the ball go. One, two, three, Prince Ali," I shouted. Arms waved, balls flew! Ten balls all at once straight ahead onto the field. By gosh, those were some of the best throw-ins I have ever seen!

It worked! They knew the motion. I put a ball in their hands. Together we combined to learn a new skill. We gathered the balls and tried again to reinforce the learning. Ten more good throws. We were there. Thank you, Prince Ali! Thank you, Aladdin!

Not only had we learned a new skill, but we had also learned a new "code word"—another one of my favorite coaching tools. From now on, when my players heard the phrase, "Prince Ali", they would know exactly what to do.

Fast forward to the next Saturday afternoon during the first game of the season. The ball goes out of bounds. The referee calls a throw-in for our team. No players respond. The referee persists. He motions for one of our players to follow him to the sideline at the point where the ball went 'out'. He leans over and gently hands the ball to our five-year-old player, Chris. He takes it and holds it in his hands. In an encouraging voice, the ref says, "Your throw." Holding the ball in front of him, the player looks up at the referee with a look of bewilderment. His look says, "My WHAT?" He stands still as the referee repeats, "Your throw". Again, the player's only response is a look of wonder. The referee begins to get frustrated and impatient since he wants the play to continue.

From the far side of the field, I have watched this short exchange between the two. I want to help my player. I want to help the referee. I know the play needs to resume. So I help the way I did in practice. I yell, "Prince Ali, Chris" to my pint-sized player thirty yards away. I repeat, "Prince Ali", and add the motion— both arms waving over my head.

You could see the proverbial light bulb go on as the young player heard my words. Oh, Prince Ali. Why didn't someone say that? Now he knew what to do. Just like practice. Feet set. Arms move together. He brought the ball behind his head and then in one motion he brought it forward and let go. The ball sailed onto the field of play, just like it was supposed to. The play resumed as the other players ran after the bouncing ball. Prince Ali! Why didn't someone just say that from the beginning?

As the play resumed, parents from both teams, turned to look at me with questioning expressions. What did he say? Prince Ali? What does that mean? What is this guy teaching my kids? But wait, it seemed to work. Maybe we'll be patient.

Later in the game the scene repeats itself. Ball out of bounds, another player is directed to the sidelines by the referee. I am ready this time. Immediately, I yell, "Prince Ali, Emily". The player looks at me and smiles. She steps to the sideline and fires the ball back into play just like her teammate had done earlier. This time the parents cheer with approval.

From then on, in the rest of our games, when it is our throw, I simply yell, "Prince Ali." This is my signal to the players. In the fast pace of the game, no long explanation or instructions are necessary. One short phrase, "Prince Ali" says it all. The player knows what to do and executes as well as a five-year-old can.

At every practice for the remainder of the season, we spend a few minutes practicing that skill. Each time, I repeat the same phrase, "Prince Ali". The players hear it; they react and perform a little better each time.

I have used this technique over and over again. In practice, I give names to certain critical skills. "Turn and burn" and "Rock and roll" are two of my favorites. In the action of the games, they provide a quick and precise call to action for those who know the code.

A frame of reference the players understand. A code word that enhances communication between player and coach. Repeated success. A connection among the players and the coach. No matter that no one else sees the picture or understands the words. We do. Our team does. Prince Ali! Nice throw!

STEPPING STONES

Some of the phrases I use come from movies like "Top Gun". A couple of my favorites are:

• "Turn and Burn" ~ turn the ball and go the other way

• "Rock and roll" ~ every one go for the goal

Shining
the
Light

"...so shall my word be that goes forth from my mouth; it shall not return to me empty, but it shall accomplish that which I purpose and prosper in the thing for which I sent it..."

—Isaiah 55[19]

Lots of people can show up and run a practice or a game. Lots of people can actually help young people improve their soccer skills. But for each of us who also accepts the larger challenge, we have a great opportunity to build character and help these young players grow into quality adults. To do that, we must find ways to shine the light on the lessons we are really trying to teach.

Devotionals

"Seek ye first his kingdom and his righteousness..."
—Matthew 6[20]

In our league, we take time for a devotional during every practice. In the overall scope of things, this may be the most important time of the whole practice.

Coaches have the opportunity to be role models. Young people may not hear anything that we tell them; but they watch every thing we do. If we exhibit qualities of character, integrity and spirituality, they will see, and they may follow.

That is why our devotionals are so important to me. I want my players to know that I believe in God, that I read the Bible and that I am not reluctant to share my beliefs with others. I try to show my players that I stand for something—my faith.

I am lucky that I have always been able to create my own devotional lessons, and I thank God for giving me the gift to communicate well. While there are other things I can not do, I can usually find a simple subject for a lesson and present it in manner that my players can understand and appreciate.

The source of some of my best devotionals and stories has been the church pulpit on Sunday morning. I'll admit it; I steal from my pastor as often as I can. On many occasions, my wife has caught me scribbling notes in my bulletin as our pastor preaches about something I think I can use in practice.

The devotionals can help you keep focused on what is really important all season long. The challenge is to not let the winning and the competition, and the need to improve skills, and the opinions of parents and opposing coaches, and your win-loss record overshadow the more valuable reasons that are most important.

How do you stay focused? It is not easy.

Consider this. When you make up your practice plan - what do you put first? By any chance, do you start with the devotion? Do you think about your prayer? Or, like so many of us, is the devotion one of the last things you do as you pull your thoughts together? Do you ask yourself, "What can I do?" "What have I done before?" "What can I do that will be easy and not take up much practice time?"

Let's try again. Let's put first things first. How about STARTING with the devotional. How about showing the importance of your devotional by preparing it first. How about making sure it will make the point that you are trying to convey. How about doing that first!

Consider building your practice around the devotional rather than building your devotional into your practice. Why not build a practice to emphasize the lesson you are trying to convey that evening? Consider how you could make the drills and the scrimmage emphasize the lesson you want the players to learn. You can do it. Please read on. I will share some examples of how I have tried.

STEPPING STONES

At practice have a "handout" for each player with the scripture quote and reference. Above it, include "READ WITH YOUR PARENTS" Hope that at least one player will follow your suggestion and share it with his parents!

Prepare a "To Do List" showing what is most important to you. Share it in a handout like this:

My "To Do" List

1. Pray
2. Share my Christian Love
3. Help someone
4. Practice corner kicks
5. Work on defense
6. Scrimmage

Then, give the players a list to fill in with the things they have to do that week:

My "To Do" List

1. Pray
2. Share my Christian Love
3. Help someone
4. _____
5. _____
6. _____

The Answer Book

"In the beginning was the Word and the Word was with God and the Word was God."

—John 1[21]

Like many children, when I was in third grade Sunday school, my church gave me a Bible as a gift. For many years, that Bible sat on a shelf; rarely touched or read. I was afraid to use it. I was afraid I would mess it up. I thought it was intended as a kind of trophy to be displayed on the book shelf (as recognition for completing third grade Sunday school, I guess).

Years later, when I started to coach, I needed to present devotionals at each practice. I needed a Bible, so I pulled out that third grade Bible. I finally realized that maybe this was a book that was intended to be used—not just displayed.

With devotionals to prepare every week, I began to read that Bible more carefully and closely than I had ever done before— looking for the right words to make my lessons work each week. I found old scripture that I knew and rediscovered others that seemed new to me.

Once I found the words I needed, I wanted to be able to find them again and again. Soon, I found out it was OK to mark the pages with pen and highlighter. Over the seasons the pages have become filled with lines, arrows, circles, and notes in the margins. As I look at these marks now, I see they resemble a road map I have drawn for myself—showing me where the next steps may be. They are directions of how to follow the path.

As I have continued to look, there seemed to be 'answers' for all the questions I ask myself. The further I looked, the more I could see how all the pieces fit together. By using the book as my instruction manual, I gained a better understanding of something I could share with others.

I began to carry the Bible everywhere—to practice and to games. It was always stuffed down in the duffle bag I carry full of my other essential coaching stuff, league manual, first aid kit, whistles, pens, and water bottles. Often I laid it on the ground, as I used my hands to explain my lessons. As the weeks went on, the book began to get dirty and show some wear.

I became concerned about preserving this thirty-year-old treasure, so to protect it, I got a piece of brightly colored construction paper and covered it—just like we used to do with our school books when I was a child.

After I covered the book, I felt a need to put a title on the outside; so, I took out my marker and prepared to write on the cover. But as I did, I felt some inspiration for another lesson. Rather than printing 'Bible' on the front, I wrote the word, 'ANSWERS'. In writing that word, I recognized that my Bible had become my "answer book". It seemed every thing I needed to know could be found somewhere inside.

A simple devotional for the players soon came together. Holding up the book at practice with 'ANSWERS' showing, I would ask if any one knew what this book was. I always get a few hasty guesses, but soon a player answered, "That is your Bible under there!" (It's nice when they are so perceptive!) "That's right, I would agree. But, it is also my ANSWER book."

I continue by explaining that I believe that the answers for my life are in this book. And, if all the answers are not here, at least, this book will tell me how to get started and point me in the right direction, like a road map! It is kind of like an instruction manual for life. It is always a good place to start. Whenever I have a question that I can not answer, I look here first. It has never failed me. I encourage the players to do the same and to look for guidance in the Bible for whatever questions they have in their lives.

STEPPING STONES

Where do you go to find the answers to your questions?

Where are you showing your players to look for their answers?

The Narrow Gate

"...For the gate is narrow and the way is hard that leads to life."
—Matthew 7[22]

I try to relate the weekly devotionals to the sport we are playing. By giving a tangible example from the game, I am often able to help the players better understand what God is trying to tell us in the Bible.

One of my favorite scripture passages is Matthew 7:13:"Enter by the narrow gate; for the gate is wide and the way is easy, that leads to destruction and those who enter by it are many. For the gate is narrow and the way is hard that leads to life and those who find it are few." Reading this scripture usually leads to a simple and straight forward discussion of how to live our lives-playing by the rules, staying inside the lines, working hard, etc. Most players have heard the lesson before in one form or another. Many of them understand already.

Now, the relevant question—how do we relate to this old passage from the Bible? What does it have to do with what we are doing here at practice?

This particular scripture fits best with basketball. As I shared earlier, I teach a system where we continually try to get the ball inside. I preach that shots should only be taken in the paint. Go up the middle. Get to the lane. Don't shoot from outside. Although it is more difficult, I teach that passing the ball and working it inside will yield a higher percentage and more points scored. It works and eventually, most of the players accept the idea.

Shift back to the scripture. Enter by the narrow gate. Work into the lane. Do not take the wide road. Don't shoot from outside. See the analogy? So do the players.

I give them a handout with a diagram of the foul lane. I draw an arrow pointing straight up the lane. The quote under beneath says, "Enter by the narrow gate". (See below) As they leave practice, the question that remains for the players is, "If this concept works in basketball, can it work in my life as well?"

Hopefully, they go away thinking about staying on the narrow path in the context of staying in school, doing their homework, getting good grades, not smoking, and not using drugs. Staying on the narrow path. It is tougher. But, the percentages are higher and the rewards will be better in the end.

STEPPING STONES

I have used a similar diagram of a soccer field, too.

Faith, Hope and Love

"So faith, hope, love abide these three..."
—1 Corinthians 13[23]

Are there other soccer lessons in the good book? When I have looked, I have found many. I am sure if you look, you will find lessons that you can use.

One I have found is the love chapter, 1 Corinthians. Most of us know this one. Remember? "Love is patient and kind. Love is not jealous or boastful; it is not arrogant or rude. Love does not insist on its own way ..." You know, the one that ends, "So, faith, hope and love abide, these three ..."?

What does this have to do with soccer? Look closely. I tell my players, if we love each other, we will play better together. Sound silly? To teenage boys? Sure. So, let's look again and break it down like a soccer play to see if it can help us.

Faith, hope, and love. The first step in success is to have faith in your teammates. You must trust that each of them is going to do the very best he can for the good of the team. If you have that kind of FAITH, it will allow you to pass the ball to your teammates.

Second, once you pass the ball, you must hope that the other player will do well. You must encourage him. You must HOPE for him just as you want him to hope for you. Team spirit. Team goals. Team work!

Third, you must LOVE your teammates no matter what they do. Good or bad. Run or fall. Score or not. Whatever they do, you must care about them. Sometimes they will succeed. Sometimes they will fail. You must love them through it all—just as you want them to support you.

Trust your teammates. Encourage them. Support them no matter what. Faith, hope, and love. Basic rules of soccer and team play. Concepts proven to work over many, many years. Where can you find these concepts? Coach Jeff says to look in the Answer Book first.

By gosh! There they are. Right in the book of Corinthians. Another page in the soccer instruction book. Another lesson in life. Another page in the Answer Book. Sometimes, you just have to know where to look!

STEPPING STONES

I have used this handout to reinforce this lesson from my Answer Book!

GO Team!

Next game:
Saturday @ 2:00 p.m.

Read with your Parents:
I Corinthians13

FAITH: Have enough faith in your teammates to pass them the ball

HOPE: Hope they will do well when they have the ball

LOVE: Love them no matter what happens!

My handouts regularly include something important the parents need to know—like the next game time or rescheduled practices; so they are conditioned to read them including the encouragement to: "Read with your parents" the scripture for the week.

Light a Candle

*"...The light shines in the darkness
and the darkness has not overcome it."*

—John 1[24]

Light a candle on a birthday cake. Make a wish. Blow it out. Light it again. Another wish. Blow it out again. Over and over the candle burns. The light shines brightly. On the cake, many candles stand for many years. Each one a symbol that life goes on. Together they represent the hope that yet another year will pass and we will be back to light the candles again. As they glow together, they encourage us to make a wish.

As I strike a match and hold the lighted candle, I say those words to my players. Then I ask, "Do you have a cake each birthday? Do you light the candles? Do you make a wish, and then blow the candles out?" Sure, we have all done that over and over again.

The candle seems always ready for us to light. Whenever we touch a match, it catches fire and begins to glow. It seems as though it would continue to burn forever, if we did not blow it out.

I say to my players that this seems a lot like God's love for us. Like the candle, it is always waiting to catch fire. Like the candle, it can burn for a long time. Like the candle, we can make wishes upon it. These acts give us hope that our prayers will come true.

I believe that each day, God lights a candle for each of us. The candle is His love for us. He wants the candle to light our way. He wants us to make wishes (prayers) on that candle so He can answer them for us. He wants the flame to be our hope for the future.

Every day, each of us makes a choice whether to accept God's love and His light. Each day we make a choice whether we will pray over that light. We make a choice whether to use the light to help us find our way. Or, like the birthday candle, we choose simply to blow out the flame and go on in the darkness.

Every birthday someone lights another candle. Every day, God lights our flame. He will continue to light candle after candle as long as we live, hoping one day we will let it burn.

Happy Birthday—Happy Day!

STEPPING STONES

"This is the day the Lord has made, let us rejoice and be glad in it!"

I get a list of all my players' birthdays.

At the practice or game closest to the birthday, singing "Happy Birthday" is the first thing we do.

I buy an inexpensive package of note cards. I send a handwritten note to each player on his birthday.

The God Ball

Put first things first.

When I went to college, I lived in a men's dormitory. Even in the 1970s, we did not have cable television, video games or the internet. When times got slow, we looked for new and different ways to amuse ourselves. One of the ways I found to pass the time was by learning how to juggle.

One day, I was looking for a new approach for a devotional. I was taking a mental inventory of skills and props that I might use to explain a point. For some reason, I thought about my juggling skills. Although they were limited, they were good. To a bunch of six and seven-year-olds, they might seem pretty amazing. I thought, juggling could be good, but how do I work in the message?

As I thought to myself, a couple of worn out phrases came to mind. We are required to juggle lots of stuff in our lives. We have to keep lots of balls in the air at once. I thought maybe the lesson was knowing what to juggle and which balls to keep in the air. That could work!

First, I took out some old tennis balls (from my shag bag). I got one for each player on the team. Then I got my marker and wrote a single word on each ball. I wrote these words on the balls: work, family, friends, play, school, money, videos, TV, and soccer. I chose the last ball carefully. All the other balls were yellow, but I had one ball that was orange. On this last ball I wrote the word, God.

At devotional time, I sat all the players in a circle. I dumped the balls on the ground and asked each to pick one up. They all scrambled for one and each held a ball tightly in his or her hand. Then, I asked the players to read me the words on their balls (this is especially exciting for the players who are just learning to read).

I asked, "Tell me what it says on your ball." The players called out the words as they showed me the writing on their balls—"Work. Play. School. Soccer." Then, I said, "What are those things?" Mostly, puzzled looks. "Not sure. That's OK." I explained, "These are the things we do in our lives. See. I go to work. You go to school. We all play soccer. Some of us play video games. We all have families. Make sense?" Heads nod. Now they all get it.

I went on, "Have you ever heard someone (like your mom or dad) say they have to juggle things in their life?" Heads nods again. "I have heard that. What does it mean anyway, coach?" "Let me see if I can explain."

First, I took the ball marked "God". I said that all my life people have been telling me I need to keep God in my life. I began tossing the ball up and down gently continuing to speak as I did. Watching the single ball go up and down, I said, keeping one thing (one ball) in the air is easy. We can all do that. With that idea, a few of the players took the ball they were holding, tossed it up and caught it confidently. I could see them thinking, "Hey, we can do that, too!"

Continuing to toss the God ball, I said, this is keeping God in your life. Juggling this ball represents all the things you do to keep God in your life, like saying your prayers, being nice to your brother and going to Sunday school.

We can all do that. Right? Sure coach.

Next step. I said, "As you get older, other things start coming into your life, too. When you are a small child, you want to play." I reached for the ball that said 'Play' on it and showed the word to the group. Now you want to play, but still keep God in your life. Can we do that? Let's see. With two hands, I tossed both the God ball and the play ball in the air at the same time, and then caught them both. I said, it's a little harder, but I can still do both things without much trouble. In fact, I can even juggle both of those balls with one hand—as I switched to juggle both balls with my right hand (for the first time showing off a bit). So far, I can juggle everything in my life.

But as you get older, new things come into your life. One day, you have to go to school. I asked the player with the ball marked "school" to hand it to me. Now I have to juggle play and school, but still keep God in my life. "Let's try that." Carefully, I put all three balls in the air. "See, I can do that, too." By this time, all eyes are on me—amazed more by the juggling than by my words. "Boy, that is something coach. I can't do that. My dad can't even do that!" I have their attention now.

As you get older, things continue to change. You trade school for work. I exchanged the balls with school and work, but resumed juggling as I continued to talk. Still, I have three things to juggle and my life is OK.

Like most people, after I worked a while, I decided to get married and to start a family. If I do, I have to make a choice. I have to put down the play ball in order to pick up the family ball. Still OK. Keep on juggling. Things have changed, but my life is still going smoothly. I can keep all those balls in the air.

Now comes the tough part. After a while, I decide that I want to make more money. So I look for ways to do that. Maybe I could work longer hours. Maybe I get a second job. Maybe I get a new job. Whatever the answer, it takes more time and energy. It is one more thing to juggle.

I ask the player holding the "money" ball to throw it up so I can put it in the rotation. One, two, three … Now! The player does as instructed. Nice toss. But the truth is I have never juggled four balls before. Not enough skill for this. All the balls go crashing down—flying in all directions, all over the ground in front of me.

Well, it is obvious I can not do that. Now I know my limits. I can not juggle four balls. So what do I do now? I still want more money and I need to keep the other things in my life. What to do?

I explained that many adults like me, make decisions to put the God ball down for the first time in their lives, so they can juggle the others. So that is what I do. I let the orange ball fall to the ground. I continue to juggle the balls marked work, family and money.

As I juggle, I speed up the rotation and lose control. The balls go flying. I pick up the balls and resume. This time the balls go high and low in an uneven pattern. I lose control again and the balls go flying again. "What's the matter?" I asked my players. "Why can't I keep the three balls going?"

Let's stop and consider the question. I stop juggling for the first time. Look at the God ball. It is different. It is a different color.

When I am juggling, I can always see it in the pattern. Because it is different, it gives me perspective. Because it is a different color, it helps me to judge the speed of all the balls. With the right perspective and the right speed, I can keep the balls going. Watch. I put down one ball and exchange it for the God ball again. I start juggling and this time the pattern and rotation are uniform and smooth like before. The God ball gives me a point of reference.

That is the reason we need the God ball. That is the reason we need to keep God in our lives. He keeps our lives even and going at the right speed. He gives us perspective. If we need to, we can exchange the other balls, but we always need to keep the God ball in the mix.

The first time I did this devotional, I had my daughter color enough God balls so that I could give each player one at the end of practice.

The next day, one of the moms told me her son had slept with his ball that night. Do you suppose he got the message? Do you suppose if we all held a God ball tightly we might let go of some of those other things we are trying to juggle?

Of all the things I learned in college, perhaps juggling was the most important after all.

STEPPING STONES

Each of us has talents.

Use those talents to teach your players.

Draw, sing, dance, play the harmonica!

A Drink of Jesus

"If any one thirst, let him come to me and drink."
—John 7²⁵

It was a hot September afternoon on the practice field. After twenty minutes of warm-ups and drills, my micro soccer players were ready for a break. I blew the whistle and yelled, "Water! Get your water bottle and bring it to the circle." Then, I added, "But don't drink, yet!!"

I got a few confused looks as the small players scurried to the bench to retrieve their bottles. Quickly they all circled around me like they always do at water break. All red-cheeked, some still panting, they were looking for me to give them permission to drink.

Before I did, I had them sit down. Calmly and quietly, I asked, "Are you thirsty?" "Yes," was the reply. I asked, "Would you like some of your water?" "Yes, yes..." "Do you think it will taste good?" "Yes, yes, can we just take a drink?" I waited another moment that seemed like forever, and then said, "I want you to remember how you feel right now ... another pause, then, "OK, have a drink".

Immediately bottles turned up and a collective sucking sound came from all around me. Slurp, slurp ... water running down chins. Then, one by one came the obligatory, "AAHH!" They had what they wanted. That tasted good.

So I asked, "Did that taste good?" How did you feel before I let you drink?" They thought a moment, then "I felt real thirsty!" "Did you feel like you wanted some water?" "Yes." "Did you think the water would make you feel better? Did you want it real bad?" "Yes. Yes."

I went on. "Why do you need water?" "We need it to live!"

"Good answer." "We have to have water or we will shrivel up and die." Right again. "You have to have water to live. Our bodies are mostly water. How often do we need water?" "All the time." "Right. We can not go very long without it. We drink water all the time."

I asked another series of questions. "Where do we get water? In our houses?" "Sure." "Where in our houses? From a faucet in the kitchen? OK. Where else? From the bottle in the refrigerator?" "Sure." "Other places? In the bathroom? From a hose outside?" The responses kept coming, "Yes, yes, yes."

"Can we find water anywhere else when we need it? At Grandma's house? At a restaurant? A drinking fountain at school?" "Yes, yes, yes." Almost anywhere we go, we can find water.

What do we drink water from? Water bottles? A glass? A bucket? Through a straw? From the hose? All those things and many more. It doesn't matter how we drink it, we just need it!

So water is something that makes us feel better. It is something that we must have to live. We feel thirsty when we need it. Because we need it so much, we have many places where we can get it all the time. And it comes to us in many forms. Water is a good thing. It is all around us. Thank goodness for water!

You know, water reminds me a lot of something else. It reminds me of Jesus. Jesus is someone that we need in our lives. He is someone we need to live good lives. When we are in need (like being thirsty) or hurting, we especially need Jesus. Jesus is a lot like water.

If you think about it, Jesus is all around us—just like water. Anywhere we go, Jesus is there, if we just know where to look. And Jesus comes in many forms. Sometimes he comes to us directly. Sometimes he comes to us in the voice of a friend. Sometimes he comes in the kindness of others. But he is always there.

Remember how you felt before I let you drink today? How your body was thirsty for something? That's kind of how it feels when you need Jesus. And then, when you reach out for him, just like you reached for the water, you feel better right away. Jesus can do that whenever we need Him.

I want you to remember about Jesus whenever you take a drink of water. I do. Look here. I showed them that I had written Jesus on the side of my own water bottle. That way, whenever, I get a drink, I am reminded that I need to reach out for Jesus, too.

At the end of practice that day, the hot, sweaty, tired players walked with parents to their cars. As they did, one small boy named Mark was heard to say to his dad, "Boy, I'm thirsty. I think I'll take a drink of Jesus!"

The water is there. All we have to do is drink!

STEPPING STONES

Do you have something that gives you encouragement and support when you need it?

What do you do when you are thirsty or need to be refreshed?

The Whistle:
From You to Your Players

"...go therefore and make disciples of all nations..."
—Matthew 28[26]

A couple of years ago, I was lucky enough to teach the Confirmation class at our church. Near the end of the year we all went on a weekend retreat. That weekend, all the participants (some 300 youth and counselors) wore nametags held by strings around their necks. During the closing worship service on Sunday morning, the leader suggested that anyone who was ready and willing to commit himself to Christ, could do so symbolically by removing the name tag and placing it on one of the crosses around the meeting room. Naturally, by the end of the service, nearly all of the participants had removed their name tags and draped them over one of the crosses. This left a strong message from each participant of their commitment to Jesus Christ.

As part of our coaching experience, I think that we should use this experience in reverse. Here are my thoughts. At the pre-season coaches' meeting, the director could place a cross in the front of the room with many whistles hanging from it.

The director could then say something like this:

"As we start this season, let us remember why we have been called here.

This place is not just a building; it is a CHURCH.

This is not just a sports league; it is a MINISTRY.

Our young people are not just players; they are CHILDREN OF GOD.

We are not just coaches; we are DISCIPLES of Jesus Christ.

Jesus said to his disciples: 'Go therefore and make disciples of all nations …' Today as a physical symbol of God's love for you, we will take a whistle from the cross and place it around your neck. Our hope is that whenever you wear it, you will be reminded of God's love for you."

Then, the question could be asked of the coaches. Those who are willing to commit themselves to the spirit of the league should come forward. As they come one at a time, the director or a pastor could lift a whistle from the cross and place it around the coach's neck.

The pastor would say something like, "As Christ has given for you, may you give also to your players. Go with the confidence and blessing of Jesus Christ".

This would be a visible symbol of what it is we are trying to do for the balance of the season. At that moment, each coach would commit himself to be a disciple of Jesus Christ on a mission for that season. Hopefully after this experience, each time the coach placed the whistle around his neck, he would be reminded of the commitment that he made in that first meeting and he would conduct himself accordingly.

From Jesus to you; from you to your players.

STEPPING STONES

Use reminders to keep you focused - whistles, hats, shirts, wristbands, etc.

I have found baseball caps with scriptural messages on them such as 'Walk by Faith'. I wear them to practice. Without saying a word, the kids notice and see a tangible reminder of Coach Jeff's faith.

One year my team gave me a cap that says, 'Coach Jeff'. Whenever I wear it, there are great expectations of my behavior.

Encouraging Others

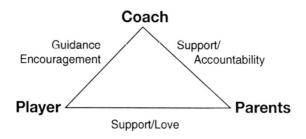

"For where there are two or three gathered in My name,
there I am in the midst of them."
—Matthew 18[27]

A coach's success in leading young people will be greatly enhanced if he is able to encourage parents (and other supporting persons) to join them on the journey. It is a three way relationship in which the coach, parents and players all support each other. The best case is for parents to understand your objectives and to follow along in a positive and supportive way. So, as I lead the children, I try to reach out for the others and take them by the hand as well.

The Good Shepherd

"...he goes out before them, and the sheep follow him,
for they know his voice."
—John 10[28]

Most parents want to be involved with their kids' sports activities and they want to show their support and enthusiasm. Unfortunately, some of those parents just do not know how to be good fans and supporters. The way professional sports have evolved in recent years, it is no wonder that fans sometimes act inappropriately. A common problem for coaches of youth sports is what I call unofficial assistant coaches. They are the overly enthusiastic parents who continually coach from the sidelines. While I always welcome involvement and interest, the wrong type of contribution can be detrimental to the individual player as well as the team as a whole.

I know that coaches have different methods of teaching and coaching their players. While all of us who do coach could do better, most of us are doing the best we can and are giving the players the best of ourselves. Most of us try to improve every season. Most of us have found a system that works for us.

What we need are parents and fans that will trust us with our methods and support us in our good intentions. What we do not need are parents and fans who work against us...intentionally or not.

Let me give you an example. When I coach boys' basketball, our offense revolves around passing the ball, working it inside and taking shots only in the paint. At practice we work on this concept over and over again. We have drills to develop our skills. As a team, we learn the concept and encourage each other to follow it.

Unfortunately, almost every season, during a game, some parents (usually dads) take it upon themselves to run the offense their way—yelling instructions to their child and others on the team from the sideline. The best example is the dad who believes his son to be a great shooter and urges him to shoot the ball nearly every time he touches it.

The young players get conflicting messages. Should they go along with what they have been taught in practice, or should they follow the instructions of the man whose attention they want most? The decision is a hard one, but the players regularly give in to the instructions of the father, regardless of how it might impact the team. This puts me in a tough position. Do I go against the instruction of the father or just ignore it and try to explain my actions to the other players who are conforming to our style of play?Or, do I just pray and wait for the quarter to be over?

One season, I decided to address the issue head on. First, I pulled out some old scripture to use in this new context. You may recall the passage, where Jesus tells about the responsibility of the shepherd as the one who guides and protects the sheep. He tells of how the sheep learn His voice and will listen for it rather than the voice of others. At practice, using the passage, I told my players that I was the shepherd of our team and they were the sheep. I told them I would guide and protect. Since I have a reputation of talking constantly during practice, it wasn't difficult for the players to understand the concept.

The second step was a stretch for me. I wrote a letter to parents to help them understand what I was trying to do. It went like this:

Dear Parents,

Today at practice we shared the story of the Good Shepherd from the book of John. In that story, Jesus tells about the shepherd and his sheep. He tells us that the shepherd's job is to care for and protect the sheep. The sheep come to know the shepherd by the sound of his voice. They follow him when they hear him call, but they will not respond to the voice of others. In this way, the flock stays together and is protected by the shepherd.

Jesus used this story to help us understand that He is the Good

Shepherd and that we must learn to identify His voice and follow Him rather than the many other voices we might hear in our lives.

We talked about how we can use this lesson on the soccer field. I told the players that I am like the shepherd of the team. My job is to guide and protect them. I told them that in our practices, they learn to recognize the sound of my voice. Even as they play intently, they can hear me. When I speak to them, I always try to be both encouraging and instructive.

As you may have noticed, in practice, I use short phrases like, "find a corner", "turn and burn", and "rock and roll" as ways to quickly communicate with them during the action of scrimmages. They have learned to respond to those cues. Together, we have learned how to help each other. This is all part of getting to know each other and becoming a team

I know there are many ways to teach and coach soccer. I have my own method. It is not perfect, but it has seemed to work for many seasons. With a couple of practices behind us, our players have responded to these methods and they are becoming successful.

On game days, I would appreciate your help. I need you all to be as encouraging as possible to as many players as possible. Please be as loud as you like. "Go Team" "Go Zach" "Nice try" "Keep up the good work" are all great cheers. A hearty round of applause at the end of each period is also welcome.

However, I would ask that you not try to direct play or be instructive during the game. If the players hear something different from you than they do from me, it can be confusing and disruptive of the flow of the game. They are listening for my voice. This is what we have practiced together.

I hope that you will trust me with the responsibility to guide them in the best way I know how. I will trust that you will bring your love and encouragement to every game.

I am looking forward to another great season of FUN!

God Bless,
Coach Jeff

I am happy to say that the letter did have an impact. That Saturday at out next game, one of the most active sideline coaches was sitting next to my wife. In the first quarter, he began to yell out instructions to our defensive players positioned in front of him. In mid-sentence, he caught himself and stopped. He turned to my wife and said, "Oops, I am not supposed to coach!"

Was it my letter? It doesn't matter. For now, the shepherd is leading our team and the Good Shepherd is still leading us all down the path ... if we are listening for His voice.

STEPPING STONES

I normally use this devotional at the practice just before the first game.

I send the letter home as a handout so parents can see it before coming to the first game.

Do you have something you need to say to your supporters?

Holding Hands

"Let the words of my mouth and the
meditation of my heart be acceptable in thy sight, O Lord,
my rock and redeemer."
—Psalm 19[29]

My wife's grandfather lived to be over eighty years old. He was happily married to the same woman for over fifty of his years. During the time that I knew him, he was a role model to me on how to be a loving husband, a wonderful father and an outstanding grandfather. In the last years of his life he told me that he and his wife spent a great deal of time together sitting in their apartment watching television. He told me that usually when they sat together, they held hands. Jokingly, he said that was part of the secret to their long successful marriage. He said that holding hands kept them from hitting each other!

In our league, before each game, we form a circle at midfield and join hands. Then, one of the coaches or the referee prays. This simple ceremony reminds us of what is truly important and allows us to thank the Lord for the blessings He has given us. It also works to put the players, coaches and fans into the right frame of mind - of fair play and good sportsmanship.

A couple of years ago, I began to invite the parents and other spectators to join the younger players and coaches in our pre-game ritual. I thought we could bring the same spirit to the fans. My idea was inspired by my grandfather-in-law. I figured if we were all holding hands, it would be much harder for us to take shots at each other.

After some encouragement, the parents of my teams began to

take the circle for granted. A simple invitation to the opposing parents was all that was needed to get them to join us as well. As I watched the parents and players join in the wider circle, I saw an opportunity to take yet another step—to use the moment for discipleship.

I thought perhaps I could interject a bit of scripture while everyone was focused on caring about each other. I looked for scripture that I thought might work. The first week, I quoted Romans 12:2 which says, "Do not be conformed to this world, but be transformed by the renewal of your mind..." Then, I added, "By coming here today, we have made a choice. We have decided not to conform to the rest of the world, but to be transformed. May we use our experience here today to continue our transformation to the way of the Lord?"

On another occasion, I used John 1:5: "The light shines in the darkness and the darkness has not overcome it". My comment that followed was "Today we can focus on the darkness or choose to see the light. I believe that the light shines upon us here on this field. Let us use the light to see all the blessings that God has given us."

Ecclesiastes has always been a good place for me to go. Once I quoted, "For every thing there is a season and a time for every purpose under heaven." I suggested, that during the week we have many things to do that keep us busy like work and school. But, this is the time for another purpose. This is our time to have fun. For the next hour, let's all put our worries and cares aside and just have fun.

I have discovered that until they experience some other league, our young players do not think we pray BEFORE the games, they think we pray AS PART OF the games. As I stand on the field week after week watching parents and their children joining hands to pray with each other, I wonder what might happen if we joined hands before other important events—like PTO meetings, board meetings, court trials and business meetings. If we prayed as a part of those meetings, I wonder if we would approach them differently? I wonder if the results would be different?

I wonder what it would be like if we focused less on winning and losing and more on helping each other. What if we focused more on our values rather than our profits? Or, if we focused more on seeking justice rather than revenge? What if we searched for equality rather than superiority? I wonder what would happen?

Perhaps the first step towards solving the problems of the world is for all of us to join in a circle and hold hands. At least if we did, it would keep us from hitting each other!

Do you think they hold hands in heaven?

STEPPING STONES

Sometimes, like during the pre-game, you have to find the courage to lead beyond your normal coaching duties.

Think of David and be BOLD.

St. Peter
and the Lollipop

Your character is who you are with the lights turned off.

Remember, that after every game for more than forty seasons, I have given each player a lollipop and talked about his or her contributions to the game. All my players and their families know this. In fact, around the league, I have a reputation for being the coach who hands out the lollipops. So, by the end of the season, all those involved with the current team understand our weekly ceremony and appreciate the significance of effort and teamwork leading to encouragement and recognition. To close the season, I have used a story based on this little ritual.

I begin by telling the group that people often ask me how I learned to coach the way I do. As an answer, I tell them that I believe God has taught me how to coach. I believe God teaches us in many ways. I tell them that recently, I had a dream where I believe God spoke to me. In that dream, he gave me advice about how to coach this team this season. I have tried to follow the lesson of that dream this season.

The dream went like this. There came a time when just like everyone else, Coach Jeff died. Fortunately, Coach Jeff went straight to heaven. When he got there, he was greeted at the pearly gates by St. Peter himself. Now in this dream, much to his surprise and delight, St. Peter was not dressed in a long flowing white robe as he is often pictured, but instead, he stood before Coach Jeff in a warm up jacket and a pair of soccer shorts, like the ones Coach usually wears to practice.

As St. Peter greeted Coach Jeff, he said the procedure was to review a few things about his life on earth before he could enter the kingdom. As he said this, instead of pulling out a stone table or scroll (like we have seen in the movies) St. Peter pulled from his pocket a crumpled up stat sheet, much like the one that Coach Jeff reads from after every game.

Standing before Coach Jeff, St. Peter began to read from the crumpled sheets. He said, "Coach, we have been watching you for your whole life, so we have written down a lot of things about you", as he showed him the pages and pages of notes.

"First", he said, "we see that you have done some bad things in your life. Not terrible things, but just some bad things like most people do. I see you said a bad word once in a while. You hurt someone's feelings here and again. And, it looks like you have told a small lie or two in you in life. But, all in all, the list doesn't look so bad. Anyway, here in heaven, we are in the business of forgiving, so we won't dwell on those things. Let's move on ..."

"Second, it looks like you have made quite a lot of mistakes. You have simply done some things wrong. For example, in school you often made mistakes on test papers. When you played football in high school, you often forgot the plays. In fact, there is a long list of boo boos here, so I could go on and on. But, we have also noted that most of the time you learned from those mistakes. You tried not to repeat them; and you often did better the second and third times you tried". Again, St. Peter said, "You know, here in heaven, we do not like to dwell on mistakes either. We like to consider them learning experiences, so there is no real point in talking about them anymore either."

St. Peter continued, "Let's move on to some of the good things you have done in your life. There is a list of those things, too—and it is fairly long." St. Peter then read from a list of good things that Coach Jeff had done in his life. Finally, he came to a point where he began to talk about the current soccer season. St. Peter said, "It says here that this season you coached a U-10 girls' soccer team. It says here that at the beginning of the season hardly any of the girls knew each other. The notes say also that at the first practice, the team wasn't very good."

St. Peter went on, "But it says you told your players from the beginning that the important thing about being a team was making new friends and working together. You told them that having fun was the most important part of playing any sport like soccer. You encouraged each of them to do their best and to improve, but you told them that contributing to the team was just as important. You encouraged them to be good sports, follow the rules, and to play fair. You encouraged them to help each other.

It says here that after every game, you talked about how each player made a contribution—no matter how small. You did not talk about the mistakes that were made, but you only talked about the positive things that each player did during the game. For their efforts, you always gave each one a lollipop.

Seeing your encouragement and your love, these players began to encourage and love each other. They made friends among themselves and came together as a team. Because they cared about each other, they pulled together as a team and success followed. They discovered that there was more to soccer than winning and losing. Because of you Coach Jeff, these young people are not just better soccer players, but they became better people.

From what I have read here, it seems to me you are the kind of person we like to have up here in heaven." With that said, St. Peter lay down his sheets, held out a sucker and in an enthusiastic voice, said, "Here's your lollipop! Come on in!"

This little story gives me a vision of how I believe God wants me to lead my players. As I gather my players in a circle at the end of each game, the story comes to my mind. As I talk about each and hand them a lollipop, I ask myself, "Am I pleasing God by my actions today? Am I living up to his expectations? Am I welcoming these players into my heart as I hope St. Peter will welcome me into heaven?"

Could the gift of a simple little lollipop be the key to the kingdom of heaven?

STEPPING STONES

Suppose someone wrote a letter to St. Peter recommending that you be admitted to heaven.

What would you like that letter to say?
1. About the way you treat people?
2. About the way you encourage team work?
3. About your character?

What are you doing to make those things come true?

Players benefit from seeing that you are not perfect. Are you willing to admit your mistakes and shortcomings to them?

Try to keep a Personal Scorecard like this every day:

Personal Scorecard

Things I did well today	Person who helped me succeed	How I showed my appreciation	What I learned and can pass on
1.			
2.			
3.			
4.			

Use your scorecard as an example and encourage your players to keep a scorecard for every game or practice.

Be There Dad!

"...and lo, I am with you always..."
—Matthew 28[30]

One day in the third grade class of a local elementary school, the teacher gave an assignment for an oral report. She said, "Next week, you will have to tell the class about one of your parents." The teacher added that if they chose, the students could bring their parent with them on the day of their presentation.

One young student named Ben was very excited. He knew that he would tell the class about his dad and that his father would surely come to be part of the project. That evening at the dinner table, Ben told his parents about the assignment and his plan to talk about his dad. He then asked his father if he would go with him on the day of the presentation. Without much thought, his dad responded that of course he would attend, and he would be proud to be there.

As the days went by and the time for the report grew nearer, Ben's dad began to grow anxious about his upcoming appearance. He knew that many of the other parents of students in Ben's class had important and high paying jobs. Some were in powerful positions and several were well-known in the community. Ben's father began to worry about how he would measure up to those other parents. On the day before the report, Ben's dad almost told him that he couldn't go to school the next day, but then he thought about his promise to his son and how excited Ben seemed, so he decided to go, despite his concerns.

The next day at school, the class listened intently as the students told about their parents one by one. The first young girl stood and told about her mother the doctor. She told about how her mother was a skilled surgeon and how she helped cure many people through surgery. The girl concluded by saying, "I know you would all like my mother. But she couldn't be here today, because she had to be with some very important patients."

The next young boy told about his father the lawyer. He told how he was a partner in one of the largest law firms in the state. He told how many people thought his dad was one of the smartest men in the whole country. He ended his report by saying, "I think you would all like my dad a lot. But he couldn't be here today. You see he had a meeting with some very important clients."

The last little girl told about her mother the banker. She told that she was a vice president for one of the largest banks in the world and how she made lots and lots of money for the customers she worked with. Similar words ended her report, " ... you'd like my mom..., she couldn't be here today, because she had to be with some very important investors"

At last, it was Ben's turn. He stood in the front of the class, well prepared and proud. As he listened to the words describing him, his father squirmed in his seat a bit—until the end. Ben finished by saying, " ... My dad doesn't have an important job; he isn't the smartest guy in the world and he doesn't make a lot of money. I think you'll like my dad, too. You'll know when you meet him today. You see, my dad is what is called a BE THERE DAD and he is here today, because he thinks I am a very important person!"

In coaching, just being there can be one of the most important things you do for your players. They know they can not have a practice or a game without an adult. They know that because you make the time to be there, they get to play. Even at a young age they appreciate that. Sometimes that is enough.

On many occasions, I have run an entire practice for a U-18 team hardly saying a thing. I let the team scrimmage for an hour. They play without the need for direction. Just being there is enough.

In my church, when we join as members, we promise to support the church with our prayers, our presence, our gifts and our service. Our presence is recognized as being as important as all the other contributions we make. The church understands that just being there is a part of what we need to do.

When you don't know what to do, you can always start by just showing up and work from there. That may be enough!

When I address parents, I tell them, that in twenty years their kids may not remember the name of this team. In twenty years they may not remember the color of the uniforms. In twenty years they may not remember how many games they won, or even remember my name! But in twenty years, they will remember that you came to the games to support them and cheer for them. And, believe it or not, someday, they will tell their children what wonderful parents Grandma and Grandpa were.

STEPPING STONES

Who are the very important people in your life?   Make a list.
Are you always there for them?

Just showing up is the most important part of each battle.

I always schedule practices on Monday evenings and then schedule my business appointments for the rest of the week.

One Very Important Person

"Love is patient and kind; love is not jealous or boastful ...
Love bears all things, believes all things, hopes all things ..."
—1 Corinthians 13[31]

When I was growing up, I played every sport for which there was a season. Although I was a fair athlete, I was not a star.

In seventh grade, I was the second string fullback on our junior high football team. Not very fast, not very big, I played rarely— when the game got out of hand one way or the other. One Thursday afternoon, we had a 4:30 p.m. game against another junior high team. As you might imagine, in seventh grade we played our games on what was normally a practice field. The only improvements were the fresh lines of chalk laid down for game day. No bleachers, no benches. Players and fans alike stood along the sidelines.

On this particular day, there was a steady rain that turned into a downpour by half time. But the game went on. This was football, after all! After warming up, I stood dutifully along the sidelines with the other subs waiting for the first string to pull ahead so we would get the chance to play those last few minutes at the end.

As the rain poured down, I looked over my shoulder to see if any fans had gathered behind us. To my surprise there were three— one kid's older brother and two dads. One of those dads was mine. Having come straight from work, he stood on the sidelines in his shirt, tie and London Fog topcoat. His was hair slicked down from the rain as he watched intently.

I knew that my dad had come to support me. He had come with the same hope I had. We hoped that as the clock wound down,

I might have my chance to get in the game a few last plays. But, whatever happened, he came to "be there". I remember turning back to watch the game, proud that my dad was one of the two that were there that day.

Since that day in seventh grade, I played many more football games, and I participated in years of other athletic events. In my life, I have been lucky enough to have had many other times of recognition and pride. Among others, I graduated from college with honors and from law school. I walked across the stage at commencement both times. But, since that fall day in seventh grade, I have never again looked over my shoulder to see if my dad was there watching. I had no need. I knew he was there. If he would stand in the pouring rain on the sideline at Lakeside Junior High School, he would always be there to support, encourage and love me. Even on the rare occasion when he was not there physically, I knew he was there spiritually.

You see, my dad wasn't the smartest man in the world, he did not make a lot of money, and he wasn't famous. But my dad was something called a "be there dad", so, for all my life I have felt like a very important person!

STEPPING STONES

Are you a presence in someone's life?

Are you fulfilling your responsibility to them?

Keeping
Your
Balance

*"Go placidly amid the noise and haste
and remember what peace there may be in silence."*
—Desiderata[32]

Despite all my good intentions, sometimes I lose perspective. Sometime during the season, things get tense, and I start to think too much about winning. Sometimes it is pressure (overt or subtle) from the parents that makes me want to try too hard to win. Sometimes it is the attitude of an overly aggressive coach on the other sideline that draws me into the fray. On more than one occasion, it has been watching an undefeated season slip away that caused my emotions to stir. On the path there are stones that are placed just to help us keep our balance. We must be able to spot them and use them to steady ourselves before we fall.

Angels Among Us

"Blessed are the meek,
for they shall inherit the earth."
—Matthew 5[33]

On every team that I have ever coached there have always been players who were there for some reason other than winning. These are the kids who truly are there just for the pure fun of it. Often they are the players who have never been on a team before and are just thrilled at the opportunity to play. Sometimes they are the players who even at a young age have realized they are not gifted as athletes and are satisfied just to be playing. Sometimes there are other reasons for their wonderful attitudes. These kids go through the season happy and content. Usually they play hard, but rarely get frustrated. They often make mistakes, but know how to laugh at themselves. They are what playing sports should be about. I call these kids my angels.

Knowing about these angels has been a critical step in my journey. Now, as each season starts, I try to identify that angel on my team. Then I use him as my compass. He helps me keep my perspective.

I'll admit. I am not perfect. I love the competition. I am weak enough to be sucked in by the glory of winning more games than I lose (and somehow thinking that my coaching has something to do with it!) When I start to slide, when I start to think about winning too much, when I start to think about changing my player rotation or putting the better players back into a close game, that player fulfills the purpose for which he was sent. At that point, he takes his place as 'an angel among us'. When I see his face, I am reminded of the more important reasons that I am there. I take a breath, a smile comes to my face, and I go back to what I know I am supposed to be doing.

Like so many other lessons, I did not figure this one out by myself. Before I knew it, angels appeared to help me understand what I did not know. One season, as I coached a U-10 team, one of my first angels appeared to me in the person of a young boy who alternatively amused and frustrated me. His name was Dexter. He was an intellectual kid. He had no real athletic ability. He had been forced to be a part of our team by parents who felt he needed some physical activity and social interaction. That was okay. In our league, we look for the opportunity to give those kids their chance to participate. But still the frustration came.

One day, our team was warming up with just a few minutes to go before game time. Dexter had not yet arrived. Then, I looked across the field, and saw Dexter walking towards us clutching what appeared to be an old towel. I shouted for him to "hustle up" and join the others in warm ups. He acknowledged my instructions, but continued to walk towards us in no particular hurry. As he approached, again I encouraged him to join the others as quickly as he could. He continued his slow steady walk across the field.

As he came nearer, I asked, "What have you got there?" "A kitten," he answered. He held the bundle down so I could see a small kitten just a few weeks old cuddled in the old towel. "They're giving them away across the street, so I got one!" he said proudly. Hearing this, all the other players broke out of their warm up drills and crowded around Dexter straining to get a look or touch the soft fur of the kitten.

Warm ups were disrupted with just a few minutes to go before the game. Whatever mood I had created to get the players ready for the game was gone. Any sense of competition was lost with the sight of Dexter and his kitten.

What should I do? I was frustrated. I was amused. I was irritated—all at once! We had a game to play! We needed to get focused! I had a plan! We might lose! Oh, what the heck! It was a kitten! I let the players look for a moment. They all gathered around and each touched the soft fur. Then, I instructed Dexter to give the kitten to his mom. In a few minutes, the game began and soon the kitten was forgotten for awhile. The team played well. I got my wish.

But that day I learned something that I have kept with me since. I learned to keep my perspective. I learned not to sweat the small stuff. What could be more important to a child, petting a kitten or scoring a goal? I wondered.

That day, as the players rode home from the game in cars with their parents and siblings, I wondered how many conversations were about the game, and how many of the questions were about getting a kitten like Dexter's? After all, Dexter said they were free. All we have to do is go back and get one! What was most important to them, anyway?

For me, an angel came with a kitten this time. Maybe God will try anything to keep me focused. He has surprised me more than once!

There have been countless other times when angels have appeared to me at opportune times in the season. Funny thing is when I find myself in those tense situations, about to make inappropriate decisions; I do not have to seek out that 'angel' to help me. He is always there. Like Dexter, he just appears. Even amidst the action of a game, that player finds his way into my field of view. As I look down the sideline, the image of his smiling face jumps up right in front of me. God knows what I need, when I need it. A gentle reminder to refocus on my priorities. God at work in my life through the presence of a child. Sound familiar? Are there angels among us? No question for me.

STEPPING STONES

Are there angels in your life? Can you recognize them?

A wise Grandma once told me, "If it won't matter in five years, don't worry about it"

I say this well-known prayer often:

The Serenity Prayer
God, grant me the serenity to accept the things I can not change;
The courage to change the things I can;
And the wisdom to know the difference.

I use this chart to make things as clear as possible:

Things I need to ACCEPT	Things I can CHANGE
1.	1.
2.	2.
3.	3.

"There's a Rock in Your Pocket"

"The Lord lives and blessed be the rock."
—Psalm 22[34]

I was going through security at a major airport not long after 9/11. Asked to empty my pockets by the security agent; I placed my car keys, loose change, money clip and comb in the plastic dish as directed. The security agent looked at the contents of the dish before she passed it through the x-ray machine, then turned towards me with a puzzled look and remarked, "You have a rock in your pocket."

"Yes I do" was my immediate response. I said, "It is a long story, but I use it for a Bible story with my girls soccer team." The attendant smiled. Although still curious, she seemed satisfied with my answer and somewhat relieved about the reason for my carrying the rock (and that it was not a potential weapon!) As I walked through the metal detector, I'm sure she was saying to herself, "That's a first. A man in a business suit with a rock in his pocket!"

Perhaps her reaction was as much about the confidence with which I answered her and the pride I showed in carrying my prize as it was about the rock itself.

A few weeks before, I had ended a soccer practice with a prayer about how good it was when we were all gathered together on the field as a team. I had urged the players to give thanks for the times we spent together. I asked them to consider how they could take the feelings of love we had for each other from the soccer field and into the "real world" during the rest of the week.

As I left the field that evening, my mind began to transition from our practice time to the many "real world" things I still had to do that evening in my office before I left on a business trip early the next morning. As I piled my soccer gear into the trunk of my car, I wondered how I could keep this feeling just as I had asked my players to do. When I glanced down at the gravel parking lot I found an answer. I reached down and picked up a rock about the size of a quarter and stuck it in my pocket.

The next day as I dressed in my gray business suit, buttoned down shirt and silk tie, I took the rock from my dresser and placed it deep in the pocket of my pants. Thereafter, it became a habit. For months, everywhere I went, I had my rock in my pocket. It became a constant reminder of what was good in my life—what was important in my life. Whenever I put my hand down in my pocket to retrieve my keys or change, my hand touched against the rock—an ever present gentle reminder.

As I grew accustomed to having my rock with me, I intentionally reached for it—at times of stress; times when I needed comfort (when an airplane was taking off); or when I needed strength (making difficult business decisions). At times I would play with it in my fingers like I have seen others do with rosary beads. I have found serenity, assurance and strength. It reminded me of my place in this world. It made me think about my special relationship with my players. With my spirit in balance, I found myself becoming more compassionate for others and, at the same time, making better decisions.

Since that day at airport security, I have had others ask me, "Why do you have a rock in your pocket?" What follows is an opportunity to share my perspective on my life and my commitment to my faith. From this unassuming prompt, I can use myself as an example of how God has worked in one person's life.

I have tried to build my life upon the rock of my faith. Along the way, I have found another stepping stone in my journey. This one I keep in my pocket!

STEPPING STONES

I also carry a key chain that says "Everybody Matters."

In my briefcase, I carry a small New Testament that belonged to my mother.

What do you carry in your "pocket"?

Scrapbooks, Sweatshirts, and Soccer Balls

"For where your treasure is, there will your heart be also."
—Matthew 6[35]

In my closet, I have a simple gray sweatshirt that has the autographs of twelve U-12 soccer players I coached several years ago. The autographs are signed in the team colors of red and blue. At the top in larger letters is written TEAM ICELAND. All the writing is fading, but the memories are not.

I wear this sweatshirt to soccer games in spring and fall when the weather is cool. It is too big for me, but I like the way it keeps me warm inside and out. Whenever I wear it, I always get questions and comments from parents and fans. Most want to know about the team and the players who signed it. Often a dad in a designer warm-up will admire mine. I wonder if he would trade the designer's signature on his for the scrawled names of my twelve-year-olds? I wonder how many others among the crowd would trade their stylish clothes for my old gray shirt?

On the bookshelf in our family room sits a photo album with Team France on the cover. A work of art, it is a scrap book, a collection of pictures put together by a team mom. The pictures inside show action shots of 6 year olds. One shows a player kicking a ball. Another shows two players smiling with arms raised after scoring a goal. Three red-cheeked players sit on a bench during a hard fought contest on a hot afternoon. A circle of players listens intently to Coach at halftime. And a last shows a prayer circle of joined hands and bowed heads. Images that will last forever.

In my office, there is a tennis ball with the word God on it.

There is a stack of award plaques, each with a team picture. The inscription is the same on each, "Let your light shine ..." A soccer ball sits in the corner. On each panel, a young player has scrawled a message and signed his or her name. They say,"I love you Coach" "You're the Best""Thank you, You're Awesome" and simply, "Love, Emily"

In a drawer, there is another scrap book. This one made by older players themselves. Each one made a page and one of the girls put them all together. Betsy, a fourteen-year-old girl who played for this Team France contributed an original poem. It goes like this:

Thanks!!!

I walk on the field with my head held high;
I know it does not matter if we win, lose or tie.

I was just there to have fun.
And I always did, even if our team was not the team that won.

All I know is that I did my best
And beat my biggest test.

Our team spirit was at the top,
And we all deserved our tootsie pop.

You are worth a million francs
But all I have to give is my thanks.

I have notes from parents and players of all ages, thanking me for taking the time to be the coach. Some are done artfully with color and style. Others are simply scribbled on pieces of paper.

Sometimes, when I need inspiration or motivation, late at night, I sit alone in my office and re-read these notes that I have read so many times before. Tears come to my eyes. My heart beats faster. I feel warm all over. I feel the love.

All these treasures are reminders of the lessons I have tried to teach. They are confirmation that some of it did stick after all.

I am not a pack rat. I regularly clean out my office and the garage. I do not keep things that are no longer useful. I am not a collector of anything. I have few treasures from my past. But on the day I die, when my children sort through the artifacts from my life; wherever I am, they will find a soccer ball, a couple of scrapbooks and a bunch of thank you notes. Perhaps they'll even find me wearing a faded sweatshirt that says, TEAM ICELAND.

STEPPING STONES

Have you defined the "treasures" in your life?

Ask your players to make two lists:

Treasures on Earth	Treasures in Heaven
1.	1.
2.	2.
3.	3.
4.	4.

Showing Them the Way

"...give and it will be given to you...For the measure you give will be the measure you get back".

—Luke 6[36]

Like the knight, I have gotten down off my horse. Through my stories I have tried to show you the steps I have taken across the water to the kingdom I dream of. You may choose to use some of my steps or you may bypass mine and find your own way.

There is little that is certain in life, but these things are true. There are children who need to be led. There are children who need to learn the lessons of life. There are many ways to teach those lessons. Soccer is one. No doubt, we all have gifts. We each can choose to use our gifts and show them the way.

So, now it is up to you. Will you choose to get down off your horse? Will you choose to do your part? Will you choose to take others by the hand? Will you choose to pass it on? Will you join in the circle that is life?

My Little Boy's Dad

"For every thing there is a season,
and a time for every matter under Heaven."
—Ecclesiastes 3[37]

When my son was about four years old, I found the following poem. My wife had it reproduced and gave it to me for Father's Day. Ever since, it has hung in my office as a constant reminder of what is really important in my life. When others read it and ask me what it means, I simply reply, "That is my perspective."

The poem goes like this:

My Little Boy's Dad

I may never be as clever as my neighbor down the street
I may never be as wealthy as some people I will meet
I may never have the fame that other men may have
But I've just got to be successful as my little boy's dad.

There are certain dreams that I cherish that I'd like to see come true;
There are things I'd like to accomplish before my working days are through
But the task my heart is set on is no mere passing fad
I've just got to be successful as my little boy's dad

It's the one job I dream of, the task I think of most
For if I fail my little boy I've nothing else to boast
For all the wealth and fame I'd gather, my fortune would be sad
If I fail to be successful as my little boy's dad

I may never come to glory, I may never gather gold
And men may count me as a failure when my business life is told.
But if my little boy can just grow up Godly, then I'll be glad
'Cause I'll know I've been successful as my little boy's dad.

A few years ago, I had to be out of town for a business meeting on a practice night. When one of my 6 year old players asked his mother why I could not be at practice, the mother explained that I had to be gone because of my job. With a questioning look, the young player responded to his mother, "What do you mean? This is Coach Jeff's job!"

What a compliment! What a responsibility! This young child thought that coaching was what I did for a living!

As I reflected upon what the mother told me, I thought, how true. I work as a lawyer to provide for my family's needs, but coaching children is what I do to put living in my life! This is what really matters.

How do you measure success? One kid at a time?

STEPPING STONES

When people ask,"What do you do", how do you respond? What if, next time you were asked, you responded,"I coach young children"?

When St, Peter asks you what you did on earth, what will your answer be?

Do you have someone that keeps you accountable for what you do?

All My Life's a Circle

"It's not what you take when you leave this world behind you;
it's what you leave behind you when you go."
—Randy Travis[38]

When I was in college, a singer/songwriter named Harry Chapin performed a wonderful song called *Circle*[39]. The lyrics go like this:

All my life's a circle

Sunrise and sundown

The moon rolls through the night time

'til the day break comes around

All my life's a circle

But I can't tell you why

Seasons spinning 'round again

The years keep rolling by

The seasons spinning 'round again. The years keep rolling by. Season after season, team after team, I keep on doing what I have been doing more than forty times before. Players come. Players go. Some of the faces change. Some stay the same.

The circle brings me back to the questions I asked myself at the beginning and continue to ask myself at the beginning of each new season. Why do I do this? Have I changed anything? Have I made a difference?

In her book, *Jesus, CEO*[40], Laurie Beth Jones writes about our journey with each other:

"In one of the movies about Indiana Jones, he and his father are pursuing the Holy Grail. After many adventures and heartaches, Indiana is finally at the precipice—about to grasp the very item he and his father have been searching for. And yet, so precarious is his position on the cliff that his father realizes if Indiana retrieves the grail, he will lose his balance and fall into the pit below. As Indiana is about to lift up the prize, his father whispers, 'Let it go'. There is a long pause, and you can see the anguish in Indiana's face. Have they come all this way for nothing? Can't he finally grasp the treasure they've been searching for? Can't he finally make his father proud of him? Another second passes, and his father takes his arm and says more firmly, 'Indiana, let it go.'

Indiana does as he is instructed and the audience gasps. It is so un-Indiana like—so un-American, so un-Hollywood—that they would come all this way for nothing. And yet almost instantly, the audience begins to realize that the trip wasn't about getting the grail. It was about spending time together on the journey - about being all tied up and facing death together and emerging with a stronger relationship. That was the prize."

There is a young man named Philip who played on my soccer and basketball teams for several years. He is the personification of all the values our league stands for. To me, he has been a player and a friend. We are so close that others have joked with me about him being my third child. We have been on a journey together. We have had our trials. We have had our successes and our failures. We have shared them together.

Not long ago, as a school assignment, he wrote the following letter. Then at practice one night, he proudly presented it to me. It was handwritten on notebook paper, folded into a small square. Unedited, just as he wrote it, the letter said:

Dear Coach,

I am writing you this letter to thank you for changing my life in a positive way. I would like to thank you for deciding to coach in our league, this includes taking time out of your life to help kids like me become better basketball and soccer players. If you have not noticed you have also made the people you've coached better people which is something that will stay with us all our life. When I grow up I want to be like you because even though you may not be that tall you have the biggest heart I have ever seen in my life. You love and care about all of the people you have coached and that is your best quality and that is the quality which I want to have. Your love, care and compassion rubs off on all the people that are around you and I am no acception to this.

During the four seasons I have been with you I have learned many new soccer and basketball skills. Without thinking about it you have taught me how to be a better, more loving and caring person and this is the thing I value more than anything that you teach me on the court. Monday's are my favorite day of the school week not because I get to play basketball but because I get to talk to you and watch you coach, encourage, support, love and care for all 12 players on the team.

My favorite memory of you will be during the spring soccer season last year when you cried at the end of the season after the game. This symbolizes all the qualities that you contain. I hope through this letter I give a small part of what you have given me back to you. After this year I will not see you on a regular bases but when I need an inspiration you will be the first person to come to mind. All the thank yous in the world can not express my gratitude to you. These four seasons with you have been the best time of my life. What you have taught me will stay with me forever.

Your pal,
Philip

I stuffed the letter in my pocket and took it home with me that evening. Anticipating what it might be about, I went to the quiet of my office, opened it and read it to myself. As I did, I could hear Philip's voice and feel his love. Tears streamed down my face. As I finished, I realized, after all, there was a prize inside all of this. I was holding it in my hand!

Philip is twenty-one years old as I write this. He has gone off to a local college. His playing days in our league are over. But, Philip has been on the journey with me. We have built a strong relationship. I have taken his hand and shown him the way. He has learned the lessons. We shared the prize. In the days ahead, he will be one of those who goes back to find the others and shows them the stepping stones across the water.

All my life's a circle. Is there a prize inside?

Why do I do this? Go ask Philip.

STEPPING STONES

Do you have a dream? Have you seen the vision of where you are going?

Can you see the path ahead?

Are you willing to get down off your horse and make a commitment?"

Epilogue:
That is Enough

*"Now faith is the assurance of things hoped for,
the conviction of things not seen."*
—Hebrews 11[41]

When I began writing this book, I wanted to make a big impact on a lot of people. I wanted to influence lots of people to go out and start helping kids. I wanted my book to be read by a broad audience. I wanted more than I deserved.

As I wrote, I realized that I did not have all the answers. I realized that I can not make a difference for everyone. I realized that I can only share what I have. I can only share what I have experienced with those who will listen and hope that it will make a difference somewhere sometime.

I discovered that I am simply a soccer coach. I coach a small group of kids each spring and fall. After all these seasons, I have touched the lives of many and I know I have made a difference for a few. However, the most important thing I discovered is that is enough. I am doing what God intended for me to do. I teach character and team work to young people on soccer fields while we all have fun. I am a disciple of Jesus Christ acting as a role model to those who still need to learn the way. That is my gift. That is enough. I am a part of the body, not all of it!

I am "OK" with who I am. I have opened enough boxes of Cracker Jack to find a few prizes, so I am satisfied. I have made a difference for at least one "Philip", so maybe I have done my part. I have been blessed more than I deserve. So, with faith, I will wait for God to lead me on...

"As you have done to the least of these...you did also to me."
—Matthew 25[42]

For more information, to order more books or to schedule a speaking appearance, contact us at:

___CJE___

Coach Jeff Enterprises

Jeffrey R. Usher

Coach Jeff Enterprises, LLC
P.O. Box 1792
Matthews, NC 28106
Jusher4reed@aol.com
office: 704-849-0664 • cell: 704-779-0069

About the Author
Jeffrey Usher a.k.a. "Coach Jeff"

Jeff Usher was born in Indiana and raised in the Midwest. A schoolboy athlete, he earned varsity letters in high school football and wrestling. Because of an admitted lack of size, speed and talent; he gave up his athletic pursuits as he went on to graduate from Purdue University and, then, earn a law degree at Wake Forest University.

Jeff was raised in the Presbyterian Church, but he and his wife became Methodists shortly after they were married. Jeff has been married to his wife, Candice for 25 years. They have a son named Zach and a daughter named Emily.

For the past 7 years, he has taught high school Sunday school. As his personal ministry, Jeff has coached over forty (40) youth soccer and basketball teams in a league sponsored by a local church. This "league of encouragement" is an outreach ministry which fields over 900 participants for spring and fall sports (soccer and baseball) and over 450 players for basketball. His sense of humor, caring attitude, and irrepressible love for life make "Coach Jeff" a favorite coach among players and parents.

References

1. 1 Samuel 17:8 Revised Standard Version

2. The United Methodist Hymnal. Nashville: The United Methodist Publishing House, 1989

3. Isaiah 41:12 RSV

4. 1 Corinthians 13:13 RSV

5. Matthew 7:7 RSV

6. Luke 3:5 RSV

7. Kipling, Rudyard. IF, 1895

8. Jones, Laurie Beth. *Jesus, CEO*. New York: Hyperion, 1995.

9. Deuteronomy 5:30

10. Proverbs 29:18 King James Version

11. Sanders, Mark D. and Sillers, Tia (2000)
I Hope You Dance recorded by Lee Ann Womack,
Nashville, MCA Nashville.

12. Mark 9:35 RSV

13. Mark 1:17 RSV

14. John 10:14

15. Psalms 100:1 KJV

16. Matthew 20:16 RSV

17. Matthew 17: 20 RSV

18. Matthew 13:13 RSV

19. Isaiah 55:11 RSV

20. Matthew 6:33 RSV

21. John 1:1 RSV

22. Matthew 7:14 RSV

23. 1 Corinthians 13:13 RSV

24. John 1:5 RSV

25. John 7:37 RSV

26. Matthew 28:19 RSV

27. Matthew 18:20 RSV

28. John 10:4 RSV

29. Psalm 19:14 RSV

30. Matthew 28:20 RSV

31. 1 Corinthians 13:4,7 RSV

32. Unknown. Desiderata, 1692

33. Matthew 5:5 RSV

34. Psalm 22: RSV

35. Matthew 6:21 RSV

36. Luke 6:38 RSV

37. Ecclesiastes 3:1 RSV

38. Johnson, Doug and Williams, Kim. (2002) Three Wooden Crosses recorded by Randy Travis on Rise and Shine, Nashville, Warner Communications.

39. Chapin, Harry. (1976) Circle, on Greatest Stories-Live recorded by Harry Chapin, New York, Warner Communications

40. Jones, Laurie Beth. *Jesus, CEO*. New York: Hyperion, 1995.

41. Hebrews 11:1 RSV

42. Matthew 25:40 RSV

LaVergne, TN USA
30 December 2009
168592LV00002B/4/A